ACTS FOR GOD

38 dramatic sketches for contemporary services

HOWARD SHIRLEY

MERIWETHER PUBLISHING LTD.
Colorado Springs, Colorado

Meriwether Publishing Ltd., Publisher
PO Box 7710
Colorado Springs, CO 80933-7710

Editor: Rhonda Wray
Cover design: Janice Melvin

Library of Congress Cataloging-in-Publication Data

Shirley, Howard, 1965-
   Acts for God : 38 dramatic sketches for contemporary services / Howard Shirley.-- 1st ed.
      p. cm.
   Includes index.
   ISBN-10: 1-56608-101-7 (pbk.)
   ISBN-13: 978-1-56608-101-6
   1. Drama in public worship. 2. Christian drama, American. I. Title.
   BV289.S55 2005
   246'.72--dc22

                                                           2005004979

                                                                CIP

   1   2   3   05   06   07

Dedication

For those who seek God.

Contents

Acknowledgments

No book happens by itself, and this one is certainly no exception. Therefore, I offer my gratitude and appreciation to all of those who played a part:

To Maurilio Amorim, who asked me to write the first one and kept asking for more.

To Dr. David Foster, for the opportunity and the encouragement to be excellent.

To the staff and volunteers of Bellevue Community Church, for combining excellence with grace-filled service and helping me discover what worship could be.

To Professor Gary Harris, Dr. Cecil Jones and the members of the Vanderbilt University Theatre group, for lighting that first dramatic spark so many years ago.

To Rocky Banks for using and directing my work, myself — and then letting me direct *you!* This book owes a great deal to your efforts and support. I will always be grateful for your friendship.

To all the actors and drama volunteers, past and present, whom I worked with at Bellevue Community Church. This book is here (and these scripts are better) because of your incredible gifts. I enjoyed serving with all of you, and many have become dear friends. I'll single out Ann Street Cavanaugh, Mike Fernandez and Linda Prater for particular friendship and encouragement over the years, but all of you have my gratitude and love.

To my editor, Rhonda Wray, and everyone at Meriwether Publishing, for the opportunity and the effort to make this book a reality.

To my Tuesday morning Men's Group, for your prayers and fellowship.

To my parents and sisters, for giving me a loving family and teaching me about my Lord so many years ago … and continuing to do so today.

To my wife, Betsy, for loving me and believing in me without fail.

To my son, Alexander, just for being you.

And last, but always first, to my Lord and Savior. May the talent you entrusted to me grow to serve your kingdom a thousand fold … and may this only be the start.

— Howard Shirley

Foreword

Given the interests and demands of people, church service planning has taken a radical shift in the twenty-first century. It's no longer enough to open the doors, have a song, a sermon and an offering, and expect people to return. These days, going to church is an experience which requires the stimulation of the mind, the heart and the emotions. One of the greatest tools that we have in our arsenal to help us create positive, repeatable, spiritual experiences for the people who attend our churches is drama. Real-life situations acted out before their very eyes, right on the stage, have a visual and an emotional impact that not only stays with people long after the service is over, but also uniquely paves the way for the sermon that follows. I've seen this happen in my own church, thanks to the talents of Howard Shirley.

In choosing to pick up and use Howard's great work, *Acts for God*, you've chosen to give your services and your sermons an extra dimension that will enhance the experience that people have in worship and allow them to experience the truth firsthand. It will give those in your congregation with acting and dramatic skills the ability to express themselves a chance to use their gifts and see the impact immediately.

I recommend this book and the dramas it contains without even reading them, because I've seen them and the impact they have had in the life of our church year after year after year. Not only is Howard a committed and dedicated follower of Jesus Christ who displays it in his family, his personal life and his public life, but Howard also has the unique insight and sensitivity for bringing spiritual issues to life in contemporary settings. As you read these dramas, you can tell they are lovingly crafted but not so fragile that you can't take them and make application in your own setting. As you use them, I know that, like me, you will want to tell as many people as possible about this great resource.

Thank you, Howard, for taking the time to put into book form these dramas that have been such a blessing for thousands at Bellevue Community Church in Nashville over the last many years.

Dr. David Foster
Founding and Senior Pastor, Bellevue Community Church
Author and Talk Show Radio Host

Introduction

Acts for God: 38 Dramatic Sketches for Contemporary Services offers churches a proven collection of compelling dramatic sketches on a wide variety of themes. These sketches are broad-based and nondenominational, applying to Christians at every level of life and every stage of their walk with God. They are ideal for seeker-targeted churches ministering to interested nonbelievers or beginning Christians who have little or no knowledge of Scripture or the principles of Christianity.

Unlike many traditional church dramas, the sketches in *Acts for God* are not simply retellings of biblical stories. They do not quote Scripture or attempt to offer solutions to the problems they present; such answers are best left to a pastor or teacher who can explore the issues in depth. Instead, these sketches are designed to inspire thought or raise questions about the topics and issues of modern life. The purpose of each sketch is to introduce a spoken message or discussion guided by a speaker or teacher who is well grounded in Scripture. Therefore, scripts from *Acts for God* are most effectively used within a complete worship service or Bible class, especially to introduce a speaker.

Each script is introduced by a synopsis, which explains the plot. The central theme is posed in the form of a question raised by the sketch. Casting information is also provided to make script selection easier for drama teams that may be limited in size. Most sketches are suitable for a wide variety of topics, and the topic suggestions are not meant to be exclusive or exhaustive.The performance times range from five to eight minutes unless otherwise noted. The props and set pieces are common household items, or they may be easily constructed with simple materials. In the majority of the scripts, you will not need special costuming. When costumes are needed they will appear in the cast list. A blackout at the conclusion of the sketches is a nice touch; however, if you do not have theatrical lighting in your sanctuary, you may end your sketches in a different manner. One option is for the characters to freeze.

The scripts are presented in alphabetical order. A Topic Index is provided to help you choose a sketch suitable for your message or service theme. Select a topic that fits the general subject area of your message. Don't be concerned if you do not see an exact fit; the topics are very broad in scope and one will likely cover your message's theme.

Aesop's Incorporated

Synopsis: The president of Aesop's Incorporated has to mediate an argument between two employees: the Tortoise and the Hare. The Hare is tired of losing every race and has resorted to "trash talking" his opponent beforehand. The Tortoise, of course, wants an apology, but the Hare demands a change in the contract. This fast moving sketch focuses on our need for accomplishment and self-worth.

Theme: Why is winning important to us?

Topics: Being a winner, losing, self-esteem, success

Type: Comedy

Cast: 1 woman, 2 men:
SUSAN — An executive with Aesop's Inc.
THE HARE — A rabbit
THE TORTOISE — A turtle

Props: Large black circle of cloth, rabbit's foot or white "furry" feather duster

Set: An office with a desk, phone and three chairs.

1   *(SUSAN sits at the desk.)*

2   SUSAN: *(On phone)* **No, tell the Fox he can't have the grapes.**

3   **That's the whole point of the story. Look, it's in his contract,**

4   **and he's got to live with it.** *(She presses the flash button, then*

5   *presses another button.)* **Are the Hare and the Tortoise here**

6   **yet? About time. Send them in.** *(HARE enters, followed by*

7   *TORTOISE, who moves slowly.)*

8   HARE: **Susan, I want you to know I came as soon as you called. I**

9   **had to wait an hour on the walking igloo here.**

10   TORTOISE: **That's "World Champion" to you, loser.**

11   SUSAN: **Let's save the pleasantries for later. Aesop's Incorporated**

12   **is not very happy with the race today. I want to know what**

13   **happened out there.**

14   HARE: **Hey, I just showed up at the starting line —** *(To TORTOISE)*

15   **on time, as usual.**

16   TORTOISE: *(Ignoring him)* **All the animals are lined up to cheer, I**

17   **step up to the line, and the director yells "Action."**

18   SUSAN: **And?**

19   TORTOISE: **And that's when he started the taunting.** *(He indicates*

20   *the HARE.)*

21   SUSAN: **Taunting?**

22   HARE: **Well, taunting is a little strong …**

23   TORTOISE: **You were taunting. My whole family is on the**

24   **sidelines, and you start tossing out insult after insult.**

25   HARE: **Hey, it's just part of the race. You gotta psyche out the**

26   **competition …**

27   TORTOISE: **Why don't you tell Susan some of your "best" lines?**

28   HARE: **Oh, I don't think that's necessary …**

29   TORTOISE: **He said my wife looked like a pith helmet.**

30   HARE: **It was a joke!**

31   TORTOISE: **But that wasn't all. Tell her about the soup incident.**

32   SUSAN: **Soup?**

33   TORTOISE: **Go on, tell her.**

34   SUSAN: **Yes, I'd love to hear this.**

35   HARE: **So I drank a can of soup before the race. Big deal. I don't**

1   know why he got all huffy about it.

2   TORTOISE: It was turtle soup.

3   SUSAN: That's horrible! How could you?

4   HARE: It wasn't really turtle soup.

5   TORTOISE: It said so on the can.

6   HARE: It was split pea and ham! I put a fake label on the can.

7   TORTOISE: He said it was my mother.

8   HARE: OK, true, but your nephew bit me!

9   SUSAN: He bit you?!

10   HARE: On the ear — look at that scar!

11   TORTOISE: He goes up to the kid, hands him some sunglasses,
12   and says, "These look like you."

13   HARE: So I handed him my sunglasses. A star gives you his shades,
14   you oughta be grateful!

15   TORTOISE: They had tortoiseshell frames!

16   HARE: So I've got style. I didn't know that would get my ear
17   chewed off by some snapping turtle!

18   SUSAN: OK, let's all calm down. Hare, I want to hear why you did
19   all this.

20   HARE: Look, you want to win, you gotta be ruthless. It's just my
21   killer instinct coming through.

22   TORTOISE: "Killer instinct"? Who are you kidding? You're a bunny!

23   HARE: *(Angry)* I am not a bunny! *(Calming down, and with snobbish*
24   *pride)* I am a hare.

25   TORTOISE: Bunny, rabbit, hare, what's the difference? You're
26   still just a herbivore. *(He says "herbivore" like it's an insult.)*
27   You don't have a killer instinct.

28   HARE: Oh, yeah? Tell that to a head of lettuce!

29   SUSAN: I think we all need to cool off.

30   TORTOISE: Look, I just want what we agreed to. My contract
31   with Aesop's Incorporated specifically states that I win the
32   race. "Slow and steady wins," that's what it says.

33   HARE: Yeah? Well, maybe I'm just a little bit tired of that contract.
34   Everywhere I go, it's "Lazy rabbit" this and "Here comes cocky
35   cottontail" that, or "Wanna take a nap, Hare?" My reputation

1   is shot. I mean, here I am, one of the fastest animals on the
2   planet, and children follow me around singing, "Beaten by a
3   turtle, beaten by a turtle." I'm tired of being treated like a loser.
4   I want the chance to prove myself in a real race, fair and square.
5   TORTOISE: Oh, right, a fair race between a hare and a tortoise.
6   That's a laugh. You won't even agree to a handicapping system.
7   HARE: What are you talking about? I already agreed to carry my
8   home with me, just like you do.
9   SUSAN: You did?
10   HARE: Yeah. Got it right here, as a matter of fact. *(He pulls out a*
11   *large circle of black fabric and holds it out so the audience can*
12   *see it. He lays it down on the stage.)* There. Home sweet home.
13   TORTOISE: See?! That's what I'm talking about, that right there.
14   HARE: What? So I travel light. I can't help it that I'm a Ferrari
15   and you're a Winnebago.
16   SUSAN: OK, I've had enough of you two. The contract stands as
17   written. Tortoise wins the race. We can't go changing the story
18   just because you're feeling like a loser, Hare.
19   HARE: Oh, that's just great. I get to go on being the butt of
20   everyone's jokes.
21   SUSAN: Hare, you're a great performer and we really don't want
22   to lose you. Here, we've got an opening in a Beatrix Potter
23   tale. I can't promise you the part, but you'll get first crack at
24   the audition.
25   HARE: Fair enough. *(To the TORTOISE)* OK, homeboy, you get to
26   keep your contract and win the race. But you better keep your
27   little legs pumping, 'cause I'm gonna make that nap real short.
28   TORTOISE: I'll do my part, bucky. Hey, just to show you there are
29   no hard feelings, I'd like to give you something for the audition.
30   HARE: *(Suspicious)* What?
31   TORTOISE: *(Pulls out a rabbit's foot key chain.)* My lucky rabbit's
32   foot. *(HARE runs Off-stage, screaming. TORTOISE follows him.)*
33   What? Was it someone you knew? *(SUSAN drops her head on*
34   *her desk.)*

Caveat Emptor, or Let the Buyer Beware

Synopsis: A new employee at an electronics store learns the ropes from an old hand who is less than honest in his dealings with a customer. The experienced salesman justifies his actions as necessary to provide for his family. The old pro's lack of integrity will come back to haunt him, as we learn that the customer he deceived was making a purchase for a "friend" — who just happened to be the experienced salesman's wife!

Theme: Is honesty important in everyday life?

Topics: Character, fraud, honesty, integrity, lying, stealing, values/morality

Type: Drama

Cast: 1 man, 3 women:
AMY FLYNN — Saleswoman in training
ARNIE BURNS — Salesman, Amy's trainer and supervisor
MARY — A customer
JEAN BURNS — Arnie's wife (optional)

Props: Notepad and pencil, calculator, cash register (or computer keyboard), several large boxes of the same size, large "Clearance" sign

Set:

A store. You will need a table or desk to act as a counter. A cash register or keyboard sits on the counter. A pencil, notepad and calculator are next to the register. A stack of boxes (the size for stereo equipment) sits at Center Stage.

1   *(AMY is trying to work the cash register but seems to be having*
2   *problems. ARNIE is carrying in the boxes. The "Clearance" sign*
3   *is on the floor.)*
4   **AMY: Arnie? I can't seem to get the register to take my passcode ...**
5   **ARNIE: It's a little tricky.** *(He puts down the boxes and steps over to*
6   *help.)* **Here, let me show you. You've got to punch in the access**
7   **code first, then the department code, and then your code.**
8   **AMY: I know. I did all that.**
9   **ARNIE:** *(Punching)* **Oh, great. The system's down again.**
10   **AMY: How do we ring up sales?**
11   **ARNIE: Happened yesterday too.** *(He indicates the pad and pencil.)*
12   **Just record the sales here and figure the tax with a calculator.**
13   **AMY: That's going to be a pain. Looks like my first day on the job**
14   **isn't going to be as easy as I'd hoped.**
15   **ARNIE: Baptism by fire. Shows what you're made of.**
16   **AMY: Can't wait.**
17   **ARNIE: Well, since the register's down, why don't you help me**
18   **stack these DVD players? The new models are coming in on**
19   **Thursday, and these have got to go.**
20   **AMY: Sure.** *(They move to stack the boxes. AMY places the sign on top*
21   *of the stack so that it faces the audience.)* **They really marked**
22   **these things down.**
23   **ARNIE: Yeah. I'd love to have one myself, but it's still too much for**
24   **my budget.**
25   **AMY: Well, somebody's going to get a bargain.**
26   **ARNIE: Goody for them. It's not going to help us any.**
27   **AMY: What do you mean?**
28   **ARNIE: Are you forgetting our commission? When the price goes**
29   **down, so does your take-home pay.**
30   **AMY: Maybe we'll just sell more.**
31   **ARNIE: At these prices, we'd need to sell more than we've got to**
32   **make up the difference. Naw, corporate's always doing this to**
33   **us. Once you've been on the floor awhile, you'll learn you've**
34   **gotta be sharp to stay ahead.**
35   **AMY: What do you mean by that?** *(CUSTOMER enters.)*

1   ARNIE: **Heads up. Customer.** *(To CUSTOMER)* **Yes, miss. Can I**
2   **help you?**
3   CUSTOMER: **Oh, hi.** My friend sent me in for a *(She looks at the*
4   *paper)* ... **I don't even know how to pronounce this. Whatever**
5   **this thing is.** *(She shows paper to ARNIE and AMY.)*
6   AMY: **Oh, you're in luck. We just —**
7   ARNIE: *(Interrupting quickly)* **Got those in stock today.** *(He turns to*
8   *pick up a box, removing the "Clearance" sign and handing it to*
9   *AMY so that the front of the sign is hidden from view.)* **They're a**
10   **little on the pricey side, but well worth it.**
11   CUSTOMER: **The price does seem a little steep, but it's what she**
12   **wants, so I'll take it.**
13   ARNIE: **I'll just carry it over to the register for you.**
14   CUSTOMER: **Do you take plastic?**
15   ARNIE: **We do, but our system's down, and for items like this we**
16   **require instant verification. There is an ATM next door, if that**
17   **would help. I can hold this at the counter for you. Here, let me**
18   **figure the price.** *(He punches the calculator's buttons.)* **With tax,**
19   **that's ... what do you know — three hundred fifty, even.**
20   CUSTOMER: **That'll work. I'll be right back.** *(She leaves.)*
21   AMY: *(Waves the sign at ARNIE.)* **Arnie, those things are on sale!**
22   **Why didn't you tell her the real price?**
23   ARNIE: **Commissions, Amy. I've got a family to look after. How**
24   **am I going to do that if corporate keeps biting into my**
25   **income? You saw the way she was dressed. She obviously has**
26   **money to burn, and she certainly didn't balk at the price.**
27   AMY: **What was all that stuff about "instant verification"? That**
28   **wasn't in my orientation meeting.**
29   ARNIE: **Plastic leaves a paper trail. With cash, we can give**
30   **ourselves the commission we would be getting if it weren't for**
31   **corporate. They're getting the profit they expect, we get our**
32   **full commission, and nobody gets hurt.**
33   AMY: **Except the customer.**
34   ARNIE: *(Takes the sign from AMY and sets it behind the register, out*
35   *of sight.)* **Oh, come on. Amy, if you're gonna do this job you'd**

1   **better start learning how the real world works. You've got to**
2   **take what you can get, because nobody's going to give it to**
3   **you. Now keep your mouth shut and you'll get your share too.**
4   **AMY: I want no part of this.**
5   **ARNIE: Have it your way.** *(Forcefully)* **But don't get in mine, got it?**
6   **Quiet, she's coming back.**
7   **CUSTOMER: All set.** *(She hands ARNIE the cash.)* **Do you gift wrap?**
8   **ARNIE: Yes, we do. I'll be happy to carry this to Customer Service**
9   **for you. Amy, you take over while I'm gone.**
10   **CUSTOMER: Oh, thank you. You've been very helpful.**
11   **ARNIE: Service is the most important part of the sale.** *(They leave*
12   *together. AMY picks up the "Clearance" sign and puts it back on*
13   *the boxes. JEAN enters.)*
14   **JEAN: Was that Arnie leaving?**
15   **AMY: Oh, yes. He'll be right back. Maybe I can help you?**
16   **JEAN: Oh no, that's all right. I'm Jean Burns— Arnie's wife.** *(They*
17   *shake hands.)*
18   **AMY: Amy Flynn.**
19   **JEAN: You don't think he suspected anything, do you?**
20   **AMY: Excuse me?**
21   **JEAN: He told me the DVD players were going on sale today, so I**
22   **sent Mary in to buy one for me.**
23   **AMY: About this tall,** *(Indicates height of the CUSTOMER)* **dark**
24   **hair, snappy dresser?**
25   **JEAN: That's her. I wanted to surprise him.**
26   **AMY: I think it will be the biggest surprise he's had in a long time.**
27   **JEAN: I know how much he wants one. He works so hard, and I**
28   **want him to get everything he deserves.**
29   **AMY: You know, Mrs. Burns, somehow I think he will.**

Coffee Talk

Synopsis: Four friends gather at a coffee shop to catch up. Each in turn is asked a question, and each responds with the truth— their lives are filled with the pains of divorce, addiction, anger and insecurity. But after each friend answers, the scene resets and the question is asked again. The second answer is a false "Everything's great!" response that hides the true pain.

Theme: Who can heal our secret hurts?

Topics: Fear of openness, friendship, fulfillment, God's love, grace, guilt, inner wounds, our need for God, personal pain

Type: Drama

Cast: 2 men, 2 women:
ALLISON
SUSAN
ALAN
JIM

Props: Tray, four large coffee mugs

Set: A coffee shop. There is a small table, a sofa, and two chairs.

15

1   *(The WOMEN sit on the sofa. JIM sits in one of the chairs. ALAN*
2   *enters carrying a tray with four large coffee mugs on it.)*
3   ALLISON: I'm glad we could get together like this. It seems like
4   old times, doesn't it?
5   SUSAN: I know. I feel like I haven't seen any of you guys in ages.
6   ALAN: OK, who had the café mocha?
7   SUSAN: That would be mine.
8   ALAN: *(Passing out mugs)* And that makes this one Jim's and, of
9   course, the café latte goes to Allison, as usual.
10   ALLISON: Why mess with perfection?
11   ALAN: Hey, Susan, good to see you.
12   SUSAN: Good to see you too, Alan.
13   ALAN: So how's Michael? It's been awhile since I've talked to you
14   two.
15   SUSAN: Michael walked out last week. Apparently, he decided that
16   the last four years of both our lives were meaningless. That's
17   the only way I can interpret it. I mean nothing to him, and I
18   guess I never meant anything to him. Which just leaves me
19   wondering if I mean anything to anybody. So, you want to
20   know how Michael is? He's selfish and confused and pathetic,
21   that's how he is. And I'm a wreck. *(They all simultaneously*
22   *drink from their coffee mugs. The lights dim, then rise again. The*
23   *characters all assume the exact positions they were in when the*
24   *question was asked the first time. The sketch continues as if the*
25   *exchange never happened, starting over at the question.)*
26   ALAN: So how's Michael? It's been awhile since I've talked to you
27   two.
28   SUSAN: Oh, you know Michael. Happy-go-lucky, not a care in the
29   world. Everything's just fine.
30   ALAN: Glad to hear it. You've got a great guy in your life.
31   SUSAN: Oh, yeah. Great. *(Quickly, as if changing the subject.)* But
32   Jim, we haven't heard from you yet. How was your day?
33   JIM: How was my day? How was my day? My day was … my day
34   was … OK, I overslept because the power went off last night.
35   So, I arrived at the office a half hour late, and my boss picks

1	that moment to step into the front lobby to greet the clients I
2	was supposed to introduce him to twenty minutes before.
3	Naturally, after lunch I get a call from the clients to say
4	they're pulling their account away from us. And that call was
5	followed by a very brief conversation with my now former
6	boss, which means not only am I going to be looking for
7	another job, I'm going to have to do it without a good work
8	reference for the past four years of my career. And to top it
9	off, this cappuccino isn't what I ordered. Great! Just great!
10	*(They all simultaneously drink from their coffee mugs. The lights*
11	*dim, then rise again. The characters all assume the exact*
12	*positions they were in when the question was asked the first time.*
13	*The sketch continues as if the exchange never happened, starting*
14	*over at the question.)*
15	ALLISON: Jim, how was your day?
16	JIM: Great! Just great! *(He looks down at his mug.)*
17	ALAN: Is something wrong with your cappuccino?
18	JIM: Uh … no, no, it's great! I was just going to make a toast.
19	SUSAN: With a cappuccino?
20	ALLISON: Better humor him.
21	JIM: Um … To Alan. The guy who has it all together! Here's to
22	you, Alan.
23	ALLISON and SUSAN: *(Together)* To Alan! Who's got it all together!
24	ALAN: I've got it all together? If you only knew how un-together
25	I really am. Do you know I get on-line late at night to visit
26	Web sites I have no business seeing? And it's almost like I
27	can't help it. Part of me wants to scrub the images from my
28	brain while the other part just keeps click, click, clicking. I
29	don't know how to change, and I'm terrified there's nobody
30	who knows how to help me change. Sure, you look at me and
31	think I've got it all together. But that's just show — just a big
32	lousy act. *(They all simultaneously drink from their coffee cups.*
33	*The lights dim, then rise again. The characters all assume the*
34	*exact positions they were in when the question was asked the first*
35	*time. The sketch continues as if the exchange never happened,*

1   *starting over at the toast.)*
2   **JIM: To Alan. The guy who has it all together! Here's to you, Alan.**
3   **ALLISON and SUSAN:** *(Together)* **To Alan! Who's got it all together!**
4   **ALAN: Thanks. It's all an act, believe me. So, Allison, what's new**
5   **in your life?**
6   **ALLISON: What's new in my life? I hate that question. Because**
7   **there is never anything new in my life. Every day I do the**
8   **same thing, and I don't even know why. I go to the same job,**
9   **talk to the same people, make the same stupid mistakes— and**
10   **drink the same café latte. I mean, what's the point? And it's**
11   **not like there's any real alternative, because everybody else is**
12   **doing the same thing. Only the titles change. And I can't even**
13   **figure out if this is something to complain about. After all, it's**
14   **a "good" life, right? I don't have big problems; I'm not sick or**
15   **poor or in prison. I even get along well with my boss. But I**
16   **can't help thinking that it's all a big waste, that there's**
17   **something missing. And something tells me your lives aren't**
18   **really any different.** *(They all simultaneously drink from their*
19   *coffee cups. The lights dim, then rise again. The characters all*
20   *assume the exact positions they were in when the question was*
21   *asked the first time. The sketch continues as if the exchange never*
22   *happened, starting over at the question.)*
23   **ALAN: So, Allison, what's new in your life?**
24   **ALLISON: Oh, nothing much. Same old, same old. Everything's**
25   **great. Just like you guys.**
26   **ALAN: Well, then, I think that calls for another toast. To us.**
27   **Because everything's great!**
28   **ALLISON, SUSAN and JIM:** *(Ad lib)* **Hear, hear! Everything's**
29   **great!** *(They ALL simultaneously drink from their coffee cups,*
30   *then are completely silent, looking at audience, while the lights*
31   *fade out, if possible.)*

Confession Hotline

Synopsis: A wife calls the "Confession Hotline" for counsel after a fight with her husband. What she receives are meaningless platitudes and a promise of confidentiality that turns out to be less than sincere. This sketch examines both our fears about seeking help for life's problems and our responsibility to respect others' confidences.

Theme: Who can you confide in?

Topics: Accountability, confidentiality among believers, our need for others, counseling fears, gossip

Type: Comedy

Cast: 2 women:
GLORIA — Phone "counselor." Polite, but can be non-functional at times.
SUSAN HALSTON (SUZY) — Worried young wife.
Unsure about the hotline, but needs someone to talk to.

Props: Pencil, notepad, two phones

Set: Desk, chair and phone for Gloria. End table and phone for Suzy.

Sound Effect: Telephone ring

1	*(The sketch opens with SUZY pacing. She comes to a decision,*
2	*picks up the phone, and dials. Phone rings.)*
3	GLORIA: *(Answers phone.)* **Hello, Confession Hotline. Spill your**
4	**guts and we'll bless your heart.**
5	SUZY: *(Nervous)* **Hi. This is Suzy.**
6	GLORIA: **Full name please.**
7	SUZY: *(Uncomfortable)* **Uh … I'm not sure I want to give that.**
8	GLORIA: **It's our policy. We like to be specific in our prayer efforts.**
9	SUZY: **Oh, all right. This is Suzy … Johnson.**
10	GLORIA: **That's not your real name, is it, deary?**
11	SUZY: *(Quickly, trying to cover)* **Sure it is.**
12	GLORIA: **Now, now. How effective is a prayer going to be if we**
13	**start off trying to tell God you're someone else?**
14	SUZY: **Oh. I hadn't thought about it that way.**
15	GLORIA: **Of course not, deary. Full name, please.** *(Pause)* **I'm waiting.**
16	SUZY: *(Deciding to risk it)* **Susan Halston.**
17	GLORIA: *(Checks a reference sheet.)* **Mrs. Susan Halston of 137**
18	**East Monroe Street?**
19	SUZY: **Look, I'm not entirely comfortable with all this information**
20	**gathering.**
21	GLORIA: **I'm just confirming your address. It's for our files, dear.**
22	SUZY: **I don't know. It feels kind of personal.**
23	GLORIA: *(Sweetly)* **Honey, it's a confession hotline. Everything**
24	**with us is gonna feel kind of personal.**
25	SUZY: **Still, I don't want this getting out …**
26	GLORIA: **You mean your name and address? Must be kind of**
27	**hard on the mailman.**
28	SUZY: **No! I mean the stuff I want to … you know, confess.**
29	GLORIA: **Oh! Don't worry, sweetheart, everything you tell goes**
30	**only to qualified prayer professionals.**
31	SUZY: **Well, I guess it's all right — since it's confidential.**
32	GLORIA: *(Noncommittal)* **Mmmm-hmmm.**
33	SUZY: **OK. Yes, that's my address.**
34	GLORIA: **Thank you, dear. Now, what is troubling your heart today?**
35	SUZY: **I just had a fight with Brian.**

1   GLORIA: *(Rapidly, functional)* I see. Boyfriend, husband, brother,
2   boss, ex-husband, ex-boyfriend, ex-boss, dog, cat, good friend,
3   co-worker, love interest or local councilman?
4   SUZY: What?
5   GLORIA: Not what, dear, *who.*
6   SUZY: *(Confused)* "Who," what?
7   GLORIA: I believe you're getting a little confused with your
8   interrogative pronouns.
9   SUZY: I don't even know what you're talking about!
10   GLORIA: *(Correcting her)* "I don't even know *whom* you're
11   talking about." Really, dear, we'll never get anywhere if you
12   can't get this straight.
13   SUZY: We're not getting anywhere now!
14   GLORIA: My point exactly.
15   SUZY: *(Confused, giving in)* What was the question?
16   GLORIA: Brian. Is he your boyfriend, husband, brother, boss ...
17   SUZY: Husband, of course!
18   GLORIA: We get all kinds, dear.
19   SUZY: I'm surprised you get anyone.
20   GLORIA: Just clearing up the red tape.
21   SUZY: There seems to be an awful lot of it.
22   GLORIA: Now, about this fight. Was there any bruising?
23   SUZY: What? No, no, none of that!
24   GLORIA: *(Eagerly)* Broken furniture, dented pots, shattered china,
25   bent flatware?
26   SUZY: It wasn't a physical fight! Just angry words.
27   GLORIA: *(Disappointed)* Oh. Well, go on then.
28   SUZY: I'm not sure I want to.
29   GLORIA: Honey, we can't help you if you don't let us know what's
30   going on.
31   SUZY: This just seems so impersonal.
32   GLORIA: I'm sorry, dear. I really do care about your concerns. If
33   I seem overly clinical, please understand that I'm just trying
34   to help you be clear with me about your experience.
35   SUZY: Well, all right. If I could just tell you what happened

1   **without the interruptions?**

2   **GLORIA: Of course, dear.**

3   **SUZY: Thank you. Like I said, Brian and I had a fight today.**

4   **GLORIA: What was the fight about?**

5   **SUZY: He was going out to play golf.**

6   **GLORIA: I see. And you don't want him to play golf.**

7   **SUZY: No, that's not it really. I don't mind the golf. It's just that**

8   **he's been going out a lot lately …**

9   **GLORIA: Uh-huh. "Going out a lot."** *(Writes it down.)*

10   **SUZY: I'm beginning to feel like the other woman, you know what**

11   **I mean?**

12   **GLORIA:** *(Writes.)* **"Other woman." Go on.**

13   **SUZY:** *(Concerned)* **Are you writing this down?**

14   **GLORIA: Just making prayer notes, dear.**

15   **SUZY: Oh. Well, I guess that's all right.**

16   **GLORIA: Please continue, dear.**

17   **SUZY: It just feels like we're becoming strangers. It's more like**

18   **we're sharing the same house than sharing a marriage.**

19   **GLORIA:** *(Writes.)* **"Stranger in your house." I'm listening.**

20   **SUZY: I thought we got married to share a life together, not just a**

21   **bedroom.**

22   **GLORIA:** *(Writes.)* **"Live together. Bedroom." I understand, dear.**

23   **SUZY: I just needed to talk to someone. I sure can't seem to talk**

24   **with Brian.**

25   **GLORIA:** *(Writes.)* **"Husband not talking."**

26   **SUZY: Don't you have anything to say to me?**

27   **GLORIA: Of course, dear. "Bless your heart."**

28   **SUZY: What? That's it?**

29   **GLORIA: Some people prefer "We'll be praying for you." It**

30   **amounts to the same thing, really.**

31   **SUZY:** *(Furious)* **You're kidding! I call you up with my problems,**

32   **and I get platitudes?**

33   **GLORIA: It's a free call, deary. What did you expect?** *(GLORIA*

34   *hangs up, then picks up her notes. Yelling to Off-stage)* **Walter!**

35   **Hold up on the prayer letter, I got a hot one!** *(Reads.)*

1   "Marriage Crisis, 137 East Monroe Street. Husband going out
2   with other woman. Wife sees strangers living together in their
3   bedroom. Husband denies allegations. Divorce certain." Is
4   that page one stuff, or what?

The Consolation Café

Synopsis: John has just lost his job and comes to the Consolation Café for, well, consolation. His menu choices are not meals, but opportunities to place his guilt onto others: his boss, his wife, his parents. Unfortunately, none of these people can take John's guilt and grief away. He ends by trying to dump his guilt on the café's violinist— but we know that's just a temporary relief.

Theme: Who can handle our guilt and grief?

Topics: Accepting Christ's forgiveness, blaming others, finding forgiveness, grief, guilt

Type: Comedy

Cast: 2 men, 1 woman, and 2 gender neutral roles:
JOHN HAMILTON — Thirties. He has just lost his job, and he is confused about his future and disappointed with his life.
MAITRE D' — Posh waiter/maitre d' in a very upscale cafe. Snooty, but polite. Speaks with a very pronounced fake French accent. Male or female.
MR. BURLMAN — John's former employer. A very patient and insightful man.
SALLY — John's wife.
VIOLINIST — A convenient target. Male or female. Needs to be able to play, or you can fake it with an Off-stage recording.

Props: Large, ornate menu; small table; elegant tablecloth; chair; violin; a twenty- or fifty-dollar bill

Set: A small table with an elegant tablecloth and a chair sit Center Stage.

1   *(The MAITRE D' is standing Stage Right of the table. The*
2   *VIOLINIST is tuning his instrument at Stage Left. JOHN enters,*
3   *looking around curiously, and tentatively approaches the*
4   *MAITRE D'. JOHN's mood is downbeat.)*
5   **JOHN: Excuse me?**
6   **MAITRE D': Oui, M'seur?**
7   **JOHN: I'd like a table, please.**
8   **MAITRE D': Oui, M'seur. This way, please.** *(Indicates table and*
9   *chair.)* **Here you are, M'seur.**
10   **JOHN: Not much of a view.**
11   **MAITRE D': Pardon me, M'seur, but we have found that for**
12   **patrons of the Consolation Café all views are essentially the**
13   **same.**
14   **JOHN:** *(Reflecting on his own situation)* **Yeah. Bleak.** *(MAITRE D'*
15   *and JOHN both sigh loudly.)*
16   **MAITRE D':** *(Abruptly)* **Menu?**
17   **JOHN: Sure. Why not?** *(He takes the menu, opens it, begins to read.)*
18   **Conscience Canapés, Remorse Remoulade, Salad du Grief ...**
19   **don't know. Look, what do you recommend?** *(While JOHN*
20   *speaks, the VIOLINIST sees him and approaches as if to play for*
21   *the customer, but the MAITRE D' shoos him away.)*
22   **MAITRE D': Recommendations are hard to make, M'seur. One's**
23   **tastes are so often dependent upon one's circumstances.** *(Says*
24   *the last word as "sur-cum-STAUN-ses," very nasal.)*
25   **JOHN: Well, my** *(Mimicking the MAITRE D')* **"circumstances"**
26   *(Back to normal)* **are that I just got fired from the job I've had**
27   **for the last five years.**
28   **MAITRE D': I see. I believe the Broiled Boss might be an**
29   **appropriate choice.**
30   **JOHN: Sounds perfect. Bring it on.**
31   **MAITRE D': Oui, M'seur.** *(Claps hands. MR. BURLMAN enters*
32   *from behind the curtain.)*
33   **BURLMAN: Hello, Hamilton. You wanted to see me?**
34   **JOHN: Mr. Burlman. I just want you to explain to me how you**
35   **could fire me like this. I've given five years of my life to this**

1   company, and I deserve an explanation.

2   BURLMAN: I suppose you do.

3   JOHN: *(Angry)* You better believe I do. I've been here slaving away

4   for you and you dump me like ... like ... like ... *(Searching)*

5   MAITRE D': Like an overcooked Châteaubriand with an American

6   wine. *(Shudders.)*

7   JOHN: *(To MAITRE D')* Thank you! Like what she said.

8   BURLMAN: John, I understand you're angry. I guess I only have

9   myself to blame.

10   JOHN: *(To MAITRE D')* This is better than I'd hoped! Excellent

11   suggestion. *(He gives the thumbs up sign to the MAITRE D'.)*

12   BURLMAN: *(Continuing)* I should have realized my mistake sooner.

13   JOHN: *(To MAITRE D')* Wonderful!

14   BURLMAN: The fact is, you simply weren't cut out for this business.

15   JOHN: *(To MAITRE D')* My compliments to the ... *(Dawns on him.*

16   *Turning to BURLMAN)* What?

17   BURLMAN: John, your first year was great, the next was fine, but

18   the last three you haven't been making the grade. We've been

19   over this before, and I've given you all the chances I can

20   afford. I'm sorry, John. *(While BURLMAN speaks, the*

21   *VIOLINIST approaches again, playing a dirge, but the MAITRE*

22   *D' again shoos him away. JOHN is stunned, sits.)*

23   MAITRE D': *(Leaning in)* Have you had enough, M'seur?

24   JOHN: *(Bleakly, as if waving everything away)* Yes, yes. Please send

25   it back.

26   MAITRE D': Oui, M'seur. *(Claps hands. BURLMAN steps behind*

27   *curtain.)*

28   JOHN: That wasn't quite what I wanted. Do you have anything else?

29   MAITRE D': Is M'seur a married man?

30   JOHN: Yes. What's that got to do with anything?

31   MAITRE D': Perhaps if M'seur would consider this little item?

32   *(Points to menu.)*

33   JOHN: *(Reads.)* Spouse a la Wrong. Hmmm. That might be just the

34   thing. I'll try it.

35   MAITRE D': Excellent choice, M'seur. *(Claps hands. SALLY*

1   *HAMILTON enters.)*

2   **SALLY: John? What's going on?**

3   **JOHN: Burlman fired me.**

4   **SALLY: Fired you? What? Why?**

5   **JOHN: He said I wasn't being productive enough.**

6   **SALLY: You hit a little slump and he fires you? Just like that?**

7   **JOHN: It wasn't a little slump, Sally! I've been under quota for**

8   **three years running. I'm lucky he kept me on this long.**

9   **SALLY: I don't understand. You never said anything about this!**

10   **JOHN: Like you were going to listen! I only took that job in the**

11   **first place because of you!**

12   **SALLY: Me? I never told you to work there!**

13   **JOHN: Oh, not in so many words, maybe, but you sure pushed me**

14   **into it.**

15   **SALLY: Pushed you?**

16   **JOHN: You wanted the new car, the club membership, the big**

17   **house in the fancy neighborhood. I was a science teacher! I**

18   **had to take that job just to keep you happy.**

19   **SALLY: John …**

20   **JOHN:** *(Attacking)* **Well, I certainly hope you're happy now! We've**

21   **got the car, the house and the club, but who knows for how**

22   **long, because now I've got no job!** *(Satisfied pause. He turns to*

23   *MAITRE D'.)* **My, that was sweet. I think I might order a**

24   **second helping.** *(The VIOLINIST sneaks over again. He starts to*

25   *play a happy little tune when SALLY suddenly starts crying. The*

26   *VIOLINIST lets the music fall off in a minor key, and hurries off.)*

27   **MAITRE D': Perhaps I should have warned M'seur about the**

28   **bitter aftertaste.**

29   **JOHN: Sally?**

30   **SALLY: How could you!?**

31   **JOHN: Honey, please don't cry!**

32   **SALLY: I never wanted you to take that job. I was happy where we**

33   **were. But to say that I pushed you into something you hated!**

34   **How could you even think that of me?** *(Crying again)*

35   **JOHN:** *(To MAITRE D', desperate)* **Please, this is all wrong. Can you**

1   bring me something else?

2   **MAITRE D':** As M'seur wishes. *(Claps hands. SALLY exits.)*

3   **JOHN:** Look, nothing you've brought me so far has consoled me at

4   all. Certainly you must have something a little more lasting?

5   **MAITRE D':** The Paternal Potage is very popular.

6   **JOHN:** Paternal Pot ... what is it?

7   **MAITRE D':** Blame-Mom-and-Dad-Soup. It is quite the rage with

8   our talk show patrons.

9   **JOHN:** Somehow I don't think that would fill me any more than

10   the spouse thing.

11   **MAITRE D':** M'seur is very wise.

12   **JOHN:** Anything else?

13   **MAITRE D':** We offer Coworker Tartare ... *(Pronounce this tar-*

14   *TAR, not TAR-ter)*

15   **JOHN:** No.

16   **MAITRE D':** Politician Pâté ...

17   **JOHN:** Tempting, but no.

18   **MAITRE D':** Mother-in-law Mariniere. *(Mare-in-YAY)*

19   **JOHN:** Not in a million years. *(The VIOLINIST approaches again*

20   *and begins playing. The MAITRE D' ignores him.)*

21   **MAITRE D':** M'seur is close to exhausting our menu.

22   **JOHN:** What about him? *(Points at VIOLINIST.)*

23   **MAITRE D':** M'seur, the violinist is not on the menu.

24   **JOHN:** I could still blame him, though.

25   **MAITRE D':** No, M'seur.

26   **JOHN:** Look, I tried blaming my boss and my wife and none of that

27   worked. Let me blame the violinist!

28   **MAITRE D':** I am sorry, M'seur, but ...

29   **JOHN:** *(Holds up a large bill.)* I really want to blame the violinist.

30   **MAITRE D':** *(Takes the bill, drops the accent.)* **Knock yourself out.**

31   *(Exits.)*

32   **JOHN:** *(Confronts VIOLINIST, yelling)* **It's all your fault!**

33   *(VIOLINIST is stunned, stops playing.)* **I feel better already.**

34   *(Exits Stage Right.)*

35   **VIOLINIST:** *(After a long pause.)* **I have got to get a different gig!**

Cuss-Control

Synopsis: An "infomercial" urges viewers to buy "Cuss-Control, the patented profanity preventer," an electric collar that shocks the wearer whenever he starts to say an obscenity. This sketch points out the futility of expecting external controls (whether social or technological) to change a man's internal character; only Christ has that power.

Theme: How does a person gain self-control?

Topics: Profanity, self-control, self-discipline, the tongue, values/morality

Type: Comedy

Cast: 3 men, 1 woman or 2 men, 2 women:
CUSSER — A man with a "profanity problem"
PITCH MAN — Television commercial spokesperson
    (male or female)
MAN — Cusser's coworker/churchgoer/golfing buddy
WOMAN — Cusser's coworker/churchgoer/wife

Props: The "Cuss-Control": A large collar with a black box or other "techie" feature. The collar should be easy to place around the neck of the Cusser (Velcro is a good idea). A large "invisible fence" dog collar makes the perfect prop.

    Several small cards, index or business card size (The "Praiser Rephraser" cards). Optional props: Two golf clubs and a hammer

Set: Three chairs set at Center Stage, side by side. The clubs and hammer (if used) should be nearby, easily accessible but not in view of the audience.

**Sound
Effects:** Tires screeching, followed by a car crash.

**Performance
Notes:** Early in the sketch Cusser should actually say the word "bleep." Later, when the collar is on, Cusser instead should make a loud noise as if shocked, which is represented in this script by the nonsense word "Gnyaa." The more exaggerated the Cusser's shock reaction, the better. Another nice touch is to include a multimedia slide show on a screen above the actors' heads. A suggested list of slides and their cues is included at the end of this script.

1   *(CUSSER, MAN and WOMAN are standing casually, as if having*
2   *a conversation. PITCH MAN stands to the side, in the darkness, or*
3   *with his/her back turned to the audience. He has the "Cuss-*
4   *Control" collar and the "Praiser Rephraser" cards in his pocket.)*
5   **MAN: And then the psychiatrist says, "That'll be fifty bucks. And**
6   **don't trip over the elephant on your way out."** *(WOMAN and*
7   *CUSSER laugh.)*
8   **CUSSER: Well, BLEEP-BLEEP! That's the most BLEEP-BLEEP**
9   **thing I've ever heard in my whole BLEEP life! You're one**
10   **funny BLEEP, Ralph.** *(The MAN and WOMAN are appalled.*
11   *CUSSER just realizes that everyone is upset, but is not sure why.)*
12   **What?** *(Lights up on PITCH MAN, or PITCH MAN turns around.*
13   *Others freeze.)*
14   **PITCH MAN: Has this ever happened to you? You're chatting**
15   **with co-workers, your spouse or, worse yet, your pastor, and**
16   **something completely inappropriate escapes your lips? Then**
17   **you need Cuss-Control,** *("Cuss-Control" slide appears)* **the**
18   **patented profanity preventer from Nu-You, Incorporated.**
19   *("From Nu-You, Inc.!" appears on slide. Holds up Cuss-Control.)*
20   **The Cuss-Control collar taps directly into your brain's**
21   **speech center,** *(Slide with outline of neck, head, and brain*
22   *appears)* **constantly monitoring your words. When the Cuss-**
23   **Control senses any phrase or word that contradicts its two**
24   **thousand-word censor list,** *("2000-word censor list!" flashes on*
25   *slide)* **the Cuss-Control immediately paralyzes** *(Red "X" and*
26   *lightning bolts appear over neck/vocal cord area)* **your vocal**
27   **cords and zaps you with a powerful but gentle dose of**
28   **electricity. Instantly the Cuss-Control renders you incapable**
29   **of offending friends, loved ones or the little old lady at the**
30   **checkout counter.**
31   **Just imagine** *("Use Cuss-Control ™ ... " slide appears)* **the**
32   **places you could make use of this amazing product:** *(MAN*
33   *and WOMAN sit down, leaving empty chair in between them.)* **At**
34   **home ...** *(" ... At home" appears on slide)*
35   **CUSSER: Junior, turn off that BLEEP-BLEEP-BLEEP rap music.**

1   **I don't see how you can listen to that filthy junk!**

2   **PITCH MAN: At sporting events ...** *(" ... At sporting events" appears*

3   *on slide)*

4   **CUSSER: Whatta ya' mean "out"?! Why, you BLEEP-BLEEP-**

5   **BLEEPITY-BLEEP-BLEEP!**

6   **PITCH MAN: Or in church ...** *(" ... At church" appears on slide.*

7   *CUSSER sits between MAN and WOMAN.)*

8   **MAN: Amen, brother!**

9   **WOMAN: Preach it!**

10   **CUSSER: BLEEP, he's good!** *(The others look at him in horror. He*

11   *realizes he has just blown it.)* **... Uh, amen?**

12   **PITCH MAN: Yes, just slip the Cuss-Control collar on, and you'll**

13   **be ready for work, play and the evening news!** *("Anywhere!"*

14   *appears on slide. He puts the Cuss-Control on CUSSER.)* **The**

15   **Cuss-Control collar** *(Clear screen)* **fits comfortably** *("Stylish"*

16   *appears on slide)* **around even the stiffest neck,** *("Comfortable"*

17   *appears on slide)* **giving prime profanity control** *("Effective"*

18   *appears on slide)* **in the most stressful situations.**

19   **CUSSER:** *(To audience)* **I used to constantly worry about offending**

20   **others. I'd open my mouth to talk about the weather, and the**

21   **next thing you know I'd see sailors running for cover. But thanks**

22   **to the Cuss-Control, I can speak freely. In fact, I can say any ...**

23   **GNYAA!** *(Reacts as if shocked, then continues as if nothing has*

24   *happened)* **... thing I please and never have to worry.**

25   **PITCH MAN: And if you order now, we'll send you as a free bonus**

26   **gift the Praiser Rephraser** *("Praiser Rephraser" slide appears)*

27   **card collection.** *(Holds up cards.)* **This selection** *("Absolutely*

28   *free!" appears on slide)* **of positive, affirming messages offers**

29   **you ready substitutes for your favorite obscenities. Just pass**

30   **'em out whenever the urge to purge strikes you.** *(Hands deck*

31   *of cards to CUSSER.)* **Use them when you watch C-SPAN.**

32   *(Clear screen, flash "Dramatization." CUSSER sits next to*

33   *WOMAN. They mime watching TV.)*

34   **CUSSER:** *(Stiffens as if shocked.)* **GNYAA!** *(He hands a card to*

35   *WOMAN.)*

1   WOMAN: *(Reading)* "Sweetheart, I disagree with that politician's
2   viewpoint." *(To CUSSER)* I don't know, dear, I think raising
3   taxes to support the arts is a good idea.
4   CUSSER: *(Stiffens as if shocked again.)* GNYAA!
5   PITCH MAN: Use them with your golfing buddy. *(CUSSER and*
6   *MAN pick up clubs. CUSSER stands next to MAN, mimes putting.)*
7   CUSSER: *(Stiffens as if shocked.)* GNYAA! *(He hands a card to MAN.)*
8   MAN: *(Reads.)* "Would you look at that? Another triple bogey." *(To*
9   *CUSSER)* I think you forgot a stroke.
10 PITCH MAN: Or just around the house: *(WOMAN hands a hammer*
11 *to CUSSER. He mimes hitting his thumb with hammer.)*
12 CUSSER: *(As if shocked for a prolonged period)* GNYAA! *(He hands*
13 *a card to WOMAN.)*
14 WOMAN: *(Reads, deadpan)* "Ow."
15 PITCH MAN: Yes, it's the amazing Cuss-Control *("Cuss-Control*™
16 *slide appears)* with the bonus Praiser Rephraser *("Praiser*
17 *Rephraser" appears)* from Nu-You! *("Nu-You!" appears)* Order
18 yours *("1-800-NO-CUSSIN" appears)* today! *(Lower)* Not
19 recommended *("Use as directed" slide appears)* for use during
20 rush hour traffic.
21 CUSSER: *(Mimes driving. Angry, as if to another driver)* Why you ...
22 *(Stiffens as if shocked)* GNYAA! *(He "steers" wildly to the sound*
23 *of tires screeching, then a car crash.)*

Optional Multimedia Presentation for "Cuss-Control"

These cues and slides are intended for use with a multimedia presentation program such as Microsoft PowerPoint. The script cues are listed first, with descriptions of each slide following.

All cues are given by the PITCH MAN. The numbers in parentheses following each cue indicate the slide or effect that should appear. The first number is the number of the slide. The number after the decimal point is the effect. For example, (3.2) would mean slide 3, effect 2. The words in bold type are your cues from the script. Click to the next slide (or effect) when those words are spoken.

CUES/SLIDES

Page 31, lines 16–19:
"... your lips? Then you need **Cuss-Control (1),**"
> **Slide 1:** *Text:* Cuss-Control™
"the patented profanity preventer from **Nu-You, Incorporated (1.1).**"
> **Effect 1.1:** *Slide in subhead text:* From Nu-You ™ Inc.!

Page 31, lines 20–28:
"The Cuss-Control collar taps directly into your **brain's speech center (2),**"
> **Slide 2:** *Clear screen. Graphic: Silhouette of a head in profile including the neck area, with an outline of a brain inside. An arrow flashes inside the brain, as if pointing at the "speech center" (it doesn't matter where the arrow points).*
"constantly monitoring your words. When the Cuss-Control senses any phrase or word that contradicts its **two thousand-word censor list (2.1),**"
> **Effect 2.1:** *Flash subhead text:* 2,000-Word Censor List!
"the Cuss-Control immediately **paralyzes (2.2)** your vocal cords and zaps you with a powerful but gentle dose of electricity."
> **Effect 2.2:** *A large red "X" appears on the neck of the silhouette, as if over the vocal cords. Lightning bolts appear, pointing to the neck.*

Page 31, lines 31–32:
"Just imagine (3) the places you could make use of this amazing product:"
> **Slide 3:** *Clear Screen. Text:* Use the Cuss-Control™. . .
> *Slide in subhead text as mentioned in following effects:*

Page 31, lines 33–34:
"At home ... (3.1)"
> **Effect 3.1:** ... at Home

Page 32, line 2:
"At sporting events ... (3.2)"
> **Effect 3.2:** ... at Sporting Events

Page 32, line 6:
"Or in church ... (3.3)"
> **Effect 3.3:** ... at Church

Page 32, lines 12–13:
"Yes, just slip the Cuss-Control collar on, and you'll be ready for work, play, and **the evening news! (3.4)"**
> **Effect 3.4:** ... *Anywhere!*

Page 32, lines 14–18:
"The Cuss-Control (4)"
> **Slide 4:** *Clear screen. Flash up bulleted text, in order:*
"collar fits **comfortably (4.1)"**
> **Effect 4.1:** • Stylish
"around even the **stiffest (4.2)"**
> **Effect 4.2:** • Comfortable
"neck, giving **prime profanity control (4.3)** in the most stressful situations."
> **Effect 4.3:** • Effective

Page 32, lines 25–28:
"And if you order now, we'll send you as a free bonus gift the **Praiser Rephraser (5)"**
> **Slide 5:** *Clear screen. Text:* Praiser Rephraser™!

"card collection. This **selection (5.1)** of ... "
Effect 5.1: *Flash subhead:* Absolutely Free!

Page 32, line 31:
"Use them when you watch **C-SPAN. (6)**"
Slide 6: *Clear screen. Flash smaller text:* (Dramatization.)

Page 33, lines 15–20:
"Yes, it's the amazing **Cuss-Control (7)**"
Slide 7: *Clear screen. Slide in Text:* Cuss-Control™!
"with the bonus **Praiser Rephraser (7.1)**"
Effect 7.1: *Slide in Text:* Praiser Rephraser™!
"from **Nu-You! (7.2)**"
Effect 7.2: *Flash Text:* Nu-You!™
"**Order yours (7.3)** today!"
Effect 7.3: *Subhead:* 1-800-NO-CUSS-N
"**Not recommended (7.4)** for use during rush hour traffic."
Effect 7.4: *Small text:* Use as directed.

The Dealmaker

Synopsis: A woman describes how as a child she learned to make deals with God. If she wanted something from God, she would offer to do something she thought he wanted in return (cleaning her room, obeying her parents). Now, as an adult, the deals have stopped working. She has nothing left to give God, and she doesn't know what he wants anymore. This sketch looks at how we try to manipulate God but fail to take advantage of the life-changing relationship he offers us.

Theme: What does God want from us?

Topics: Attitudes about God, bargaining with God, earning God's favor, faith vs. works, grace, relationship with God

Type: Drama

Cast: 1 woman:
THERESE

Props: None

Set: Bare stage

1   (THERESE enters.)
2   THERESE: I'm a dealmaker. I make deals with God. If I need
3   something, I just promise God something and hope he keeps
4   up his end. Don't look at me funny, because I know you do it
5   too.
6   It all started when I was seven. My cat, Mr. Googlepuss, got
7   sick. My friend Josie said he was going to die. Josie was eight,
8   so she knew everything. Josie told me that God could make
9   Mr. Googlepuss well, but that I'd have to give God something
10   he wanted. It sounded right to me. After all, Josie was eight, so
11   she should know.
12   So I made a deal with God. I'd be a good little girl. I wouldn't
13   talk back to Mom. I'd clean my plate— even the broccoli. And
14   I'd make my bed almost every day without being asked. And
15   he'd make sure that Mr. Googlepuss didn't die.
16   And it worked. Mr. Googlepuss didn't die. Of course, I did
17   have to change his name to Mrs. Googlepuss, and Mom had to
18   find a home for all the kittens, but God kept up his end of the
19   bargain and I kept up mine. Most of the time, anyway.
20   So I figured that this bargain stuff must work pretty well.
21   From then on, whenever I needed something from God, I'd
22   simply make another bargain. When I needed to pass a math
23   test, I'd make a bargain with God . When I needed to sneak in
24   after a late night date without Dad hearing, I'd make a bargain
25   with God. I got to be an expert dealmaker. Give me this, God,
26   and I'll give you that. And all my little deals seemed to work.
27   It seemed like Josie was right. You want something, you
28   bargain for it. Only Josie never told me what to do when God
29   didn't keep up his end of the bargain. Because now I know
30   that he doesn't. Now, when I really need those bargains ...
31   when I need the deals to work, they don't.
32   My bargains didn't save my marriage. My bargains didn't ...
33   didn't keep Dad alive. And now ... now I don't even know
34   what God wants anymore. When I was seven it was easy.
35   Clean my room. Don't sass the teachers. Stop kicking my

1   brother. But now ... now I try everything, and nothing works.
2   And I don't have anything left to bargain with. And I don't
3   know if I'd even try if I did.
4   Well, I'm through with bargains and deals. If God wants
5   something from me, he's got to tell me what it is, or he's just
6   got to do it himself. Because I've got nothing left. Nothing left
7   but me. And I'm scared that's what he really wants.

The Door

Synopsis: The sketch begins as a husband and wife end a fight by slamming a door between them. We then hear each one talk about the struggle their marriage has become. The effect is a duet monolog. Each says a line in turn, talking independently but following the same thought. At the end, both wonder how they can heal the rift between them and open the door.

Theme: How do we deal with stress in our marriages?

Topics: Divorce, marital problems, marriage, relationships

Type: Drama

Cast: 1 man, 1 woman:
HE — A husband
SHE — A wife

Props: None

Set: A door inside a frame, placed at Center Stage so it faces the audience. The door should be freestanding and functional, sturdy enough to be slammed shut without moving.

1   *(HE and SHE are both on the "inside" of the door, unseen by the*
2   *audience. The door is closed.)*
3   **HE: That's it! I'm not going to listen to this anymore!** *(HE opens*
4   *the door and walks through.)*
5   **SHE:** *(Leans through to yell after him.)* **Fine! I don't know why I**
6   **bother to try and talk to you!** *(SHE slams the door angrily, then*
7   *steps around in front of the door. Both walk away from the door and*
8   *step forward to speak to the audience. Throughout the play, neither*
9   *reacts to or acknowledges the presence of the other On-stage.)*
10 **HE: I just had a fight with my wife.**
11 **SHE: Bill and I have been fighting a lot lately.**
12 **HE: I don't really know how it started.**
13 **SHE: It doesn't seem to matter what we fight about.**
14 **HE: But once we get started, I know how each fight is going to end.**
15 **BOTH: All our fights end the same way.** *(They look at the door.)*
16 **SHE: He'll say something, then I'll say something, and the next**
17 **thing you know, one of us is slamming the door.**
18 **HE: It just seems easier to let the air clear for a few days.**
19 **SHE: When Bill's not here, I do calm down a little.**
20 **HE: Then I come back, and things seem good for a while.**
21 **SHE: But it never lasts. The same old arguments start again ...**
22 **HE: Pretty soon, she's yelling, and I'm shouting ...**
23 **BOTH:** *(Looking back at the door)* **... and then the door slams.**
24 **HE: I don't really know how we got here.**
25 **SHE: We didn't fight when we were dating.**
26 **HE: OK, so we started out with a squabble or two.**
27 **SHE: Except for that argument about his "friend," Hank.**
28 **HE: She didn't like my college roommate at first. But I think she**
29 **finally accepted Hank for who he was.**
30 **SHE: Boy, was he a jerk!**
31 **HE: Of course, I don't really remember our first fight as a couple ...**
32 **SHE: Then there was the "Meat Loaf Incident."**
33 **HE: Oh, yeah. A month after the honeymoon, I mentioned that I**
34 **liked a little more spice in my meat loaf.**
35 **SHE: He told me I didn't cook the meat loaf as well as his mother.**

1   HE: Man, did she ever blow that out of proportion.

2   SHE: So I calmly picked up the meat loaf ...

3   HE: The next thing I know she opens the back door ...

4   SHE: ... and set it on the patio for the dog.

5   HE: ... and flings the whole meat loaf into the backyard, splat on

6   the patio.

7   SHE: That dog had the best meal of his life.

8   HE: Gulliver walked over, sniffed it, and trotted back to his dry

9   dog food. I had to scrape the meat loaf up the next morning

10   with a shovel.

11 SHE: But those fights were nothing like the ones we have now.

12 HE: Newlywed spats I can handle. But these shouting matches ...

13 SHE: You don't walk out the door over a meat loaf.

14 HE: I have to leave just so I can think.

15 SHE: I don't know if I could tell you why you do walk out the door.

16 HE: Somehow I think if I can just put that door between us for a

17   while, I'll be able to figure out what's going on.

18 SHE: After the door slams, all you're left with is anger and resentment.

19 HE: But I never can. Oh, I can find a thousand ways to blame her

20   for what's going on.

21 SHE: You tell yourself that it's all his fault.

22 HE: But I know that isn't the truth. Not really.

23 SHE: It's easy to lie to a door.

24 HE: Every time that door closes, it gets harder and harder to open

25   again.

26 SHE: Each time that door slams, I wonder if it's the last time.

27 HE: You think, "Wouldn't it be easier to just walk away?"

28 SHE: Sometimes I tell myself that's what I want.

29 HE: As if walking away would make everything right.

30 SHE: But that's a lie too.

31 HE: So I stand here and stare at a closed door.

32 SHE: I ask myself, why do I keep closing the door?

33 HE: When what I want to do ...

34 SHE: What I really want to do ...

35 BOTH: ... is open it. *(They look back at the door.)*

Double-header

Synopsis: Two coaches have different approaches to leading their teams. One berates and belittles his players, while the other offers positive words and loving support. We see their opening pep talks, then watch the results of their leadership as the game begins — and see how they respond.

Theme: How do you bring out the best in others?

Topics: Encouraging others, parenting, the power of positive words, relating to others, the tongue

Type: Comedy

Cast: 2 men:
COACH MALWAY — Little League coach. Couldn't encourage Willie Mays.
COACH GODWIN — Little League coach. Loves the game, loves his team.

Props: Pencil, clipboard

Set: Bare stage. Two dugouts at a Little League game. After talking briefly, the coaches part to deliver their lines to the audience, as if to their teams.

```
1      (MALWAY stands Center Stage, eyeing the field [toward the
2      audience, Stage Right], shaking his head and making notes on a
3      clipboard. GODWIN approaches him, backing toward him as if
4      looking toward the opposite side of the field [audience, Stage Left].)
5  GODWIN: (Calling out into the audience, as if to his team.) Good catch,
6      Bobby! That's the spirit! (Turns to see MALWAY.) Hello, Malway.
7  MALWAY: Godwin.
8  GODWIN: Good day for baseball, don't you think?
9  MALWAY: Good as any. So, you think your boys are ready?
10 GODWIN: (Chuckling) They're certainly excited enough. (Warmly)
11     What great kids.
12 MALWAY: Hmmph. Well, they better be great players if they
13     wanna take on a team coached by me.
14 GODWIN: I'll just be happy if they do their best.
15 MALWAY: Whatever. My boys know I expect 'em to win.
16 GODWIN: Well, best of luck. (Extends hand.)
17 MALWAY: Yeah. (Shakes quickly; they part. To audience, as if to
18     team) All right, you bums! Get over here!
19 GODWIN: (To audience, as if to team.) Gather round, guys!
20 MALWAY: This is it, the big one. And just 'cause you guys are in
21     fourth grade doesn't mean you can blow it like last time, ya'
22     hear?
23 GODWIN: Now you all know how important this game is. But the
24     main thing is, I want you to do your best.
25 MALWAY: So listen up, 'cause I hate having to repeat things just
26     'cause some numskull was gazing at the daisies when he
27     shoulda been listening. Got that, Joey?
28 GODWIN: We do have a few things to go over before the game, so
29     pay attention.
30 MALWAY: I said, "Got that, Joey?" Good. 'Cause I better not
31     catch you daydreaming out in left field again, you hear me?
32 GODWIN: Bobby, you're one of our best fielders, and you're going
33     to be crucial against their power hitters. So stay on your toes
34     and keep a sharp eye on the ball.
35 MALWAY: Where's Wilson? Get up here. Looks like Peterson's
```

1   still out with the flu, so unfortunately I gotta start you instead.
2   Try to keep the ball over the plate, will ya?
3   GODWIN: Jamie? You did really well closing out the last game.
4   Think you're up to starting this one? Good. Allan, that means
5   you're our closer, so keep that arm ready.
6   MALWAY: And none of that fancy stuff, Wilson. I've seen your
7   curve and it stinks. Just sling fast ones and pray their hitters
8   can't see straight.
9   GODWIN: OK, Ben, you're our lead-off hitter. I've been watching
10   you in practice, and you're swinging smooth. Just keep your
11   eye on the ball, and you'll be hitting home runs today.
12   MALWAY: There you are, Brown. How I got stuck with you, I'll
13   never know. Look, if the ball comes your way, let Jackson get
14   it. Your job is just to get out of the way, OK?
15   GODWIN: That's about it. You guys have been working hard and
16   I know you're ready. So let's get out there and show 'em what
17   you can do!
18   MALWAY: There ain't nothing else I can tell you losers that you'd
19   listen to anyway. Now get out there and kick some tail! *(Both*
20   *COACHES now react as if they are watching the game in progress.)*
21   GODWIN: *(Yelling)* OK, Ben, just like in practice. Head up, watch
22   the ball, swing if it's good!
23   MALWAY: *(Yelling)* Wilson! Remember, no fancy stuff!
24   GODWIN: *(Reacts to a strike.)* That's all right, Ben. Get ready for
25   the next one.
26   MALWAY: *(Yelling)* I said no fancy stuff! Don't get cocky! *(Both*
27   *react to a high-flying hit, watching it arc across the sky.)*
28   GODWIN: Go, Ben! Run, run, run!
29   MALWAY: Jackson! Get it! Run, run, run! *(Sees something he doesn't*
30   *like.)* Brown! What are you doing? Stay back! Stay back!
31   GODWIN: Whoa! Stay! Stay! Good hit, Ben! That was great!
32   MALWAY: *(Disaster. Brown blocks Jackson and the ball hits the*
33   *ground.)* **Brown!** *(Angry)* Oh, that's great! Just great! *(As if*
34   *yelling to player)* How hard is it to run away from the
35   ball? Moron!

1   GODWIN: Way to run, Ben! *(As if to next player)* **Michael, you're**
2   **up. Think you can bring Ben home? Attaboy!**
3   MALWAY: **Wilson! That boy better not make it home! You hear**
4   **me, Wilson? Just throw the ball!**
5   GODWIN: **Remember, keep your eye on the ball, Michael! Don't**
6   **just swing at anything!**
7   MALWAY: *(Reacts to a ball.)* **What are you doing out there? Can't**
8   **you throw anything?**
9   GODWIN: **Good eye, Michael!**
10 MALWAY: *(Ball two)* **Wilson! Is that how I told you to throw? You're**
11 **flailing around like a dying chicken! Now get it together!**
12 GODWIN: **Way to keep it together, Michael!**
13 MALWAY: *(Ball three)* **Wilson! Stop fooling around!**
14 GODWIN: **That's right, Michael! Don't fool around with the bad**
15 **ones!**
16 MALWAY: *(Ball four)* **A walk!?! You throw a walk in the first**
17 **inning?! What are you thinking?**
18 GODWIN: **Way to keep a cool head, Michael! All right! Bobby,**
19 **you're on.**
20 MALWAY: **Screw up again, Wilson, and you're out of here!** *(A hit.*
21 *They follow it.)*
22 GODWIN: **Whoa, Bobby! That'll wake 'em up!**
23 MALWAY: **Joey! Joey! Wake up!** *Joey! (The ball sails completely by*
24 *Joey.)* **I don't believe it! Jackson! Get that ball!**
25 GODWIN: **All right, Ben! Run, run, run! Come on home, Michael!**
26 MALWAY: **No, not that way! Throw it to home! Throw it to home!**
27 GODWIN: **Come on, come on, come on! You can make it, Bobby!**
28 MALWAY: *I said home, you idiot!*
29 GODWIN: **Home run! Way to go, Bobby!**
30 MALWAY: *No! (Throws down clipboard. Beat.)*
31 TOGETHER: *(GODWIN excited, MALWAY frustrated)* **What did I**
32 **do to deserve such a team?!**

Double-O-Heaven

Synopsis: A heavenly "special operations" team has to select three human agents to carry out some very important missions for "the Chairman" (God). Unfortunately, their agents are an elderly fugitive, a woman of ill repute and a teenage boy. The angels wonder how they can expect success from such a team of obvious losers as Moses, Rahab and David. This sketch illustrates the truths that God indeed is "strong in our weaknesses," and that no one is outside of his love or purpose.

Theme: Can God use imperfect people?

Topics: God's purpose for us, our value to God, self-worth, success, weaknesses, the world's view vs. God's view

Type: Comedy

Cast: 3 men, 1 woman (Roles can be easily mixed):
MIKE — An angel (MICHAEL)
RAFE — An angel (RAPHAEL)
GABE — An angel (GABRIEL)
SHERRY — An angel (Call her SHARIEL if you like.)

Props: Several file folders

Set: A meeting room. Possibly a podium and three chairs, or a conference table with four chairs.

1   *(RAFE, GABE and SHERRY are sitting in the chairs, chatting.*

2   *They have folders on their laps. All the ANGELS are wearing*

3   *conservative business attire. MIKE enters, carrying several*

4   *folders. He walks to the podium and raps on it for attention. The*

5   *ANGELS quiet down to listen.)*

6   MIKE: OK, listen up, people! As you know, the Chairman is

7   fielding requests for our assistance from all over the globe. He

8   wants to get a team in place to deal with these requests ASAP.

9   Our job is to select the men ... and women — we're equal

10   opportunity here — to head these projects.

11   RAFE: Sir, if we could just send one of our ...

12   MIKE: I know what you're going to say, Rafe. You already know

13   what the Chairman's position is on this issue. We go strictly

14   with local agents — people who know the lay of the land.

15   RAFE: Mike, you know our local recruiting efforts have had

16   limited results. We've got trained personnel here who can do

17   so much more ...

18   MIKE: Rafe, this isn't up for discussion. In-house personnel can only

19   be sent with a direct order from the Chairman. Or does anybody

20   here really want to repeat the Project Serpent disaster? *(GABE,*

21   *RAFE and SHERRY look around uncomfortably.)*

22   MIKE: Fine. Our most pressing concern is the Egypt situation.

23   We're being flooded with requests, and the Chairman is ready

24   to move on this. *(Hands out folders.)* He's put together a plan

25   of action, code named Mass Exit. This one is big, folks, and

26   will set the tone for our operations for years to come. We need

27   a top-notch agent to pull this one off. Who have we got in

28   place? Gabe?

29   GABE: Agent M.

30   ALL: *(Except GABE and MIKE)* **Moses?!**

31   RAFE: That's it?

32   SHERRY: You've got to be kidding. I thought we wrote him off

33   years ago.

34   GABE: Nope. He still heads the list.

35   RAFE: This is a joke. He's a complete washout!

1 GABE: He knows the client situation intimately, he's well-
2   educated, he's got experience with the local government, not
3   to mention high-level connections ...
4 SHERRY: Gabe, his experience is fifty years behind the times! And
5   he's done nothing to maintain those connections since he split
6   the scene.
7 RAFE: Yeah, let's talk about that. The man's on the lam from a
8   possible murder charge, and you're wanting to use him as the
9   point man for this project?
10 GABE: The Chairman seems to think there were extenuating
11   circumstances behind the incident that warrant a second
12   chance.
13 MIKE: OK, we're not going to argue with the Chairman, folks. So
14   where is Agent M now?
15 GABE: *(Looks in a folder.)* According to our latest intelligence, he's
16   living in the desert, across the Egyptian border.
17 RAFE: Oh, good grief.
18 SHERRY: Wait a minute, this might not be so bad. After all, he's
19   had to have known something like this was in the works. So
20   what's he been doing? Establishing a base of operations,
21   right? Building up a clandestine resistance movement?
22 GABE: Um, no. Says here he's been herding sheep.
23 ALL: *(Except GABE) Herding sheep?!*
24 RAFE: The man's got a poli-sci degree from the leading university
25   in Egypt, and he's herding sheep?
26 SHERRY: Now hold on. A little business experience isn't a bad
27   thing. It shows leadership ability and initiative. So how long
28   has he been running this business?
29 GABE: Well, it's not actually his business. He, um, works for his
30   father-in-law.
31 RAFE and SHERRY: Loser! *(They string the word out: "Looo-zerr!")*
32 MIKE: That's enough, people! The Chairman supports this
33   project, and I expect all of you to get on board, is that clear?
34 RAFE and SHERRY: Yes, sir.
35 MIKE: *(Recovering from his surprise)* OK. Well. I don't think any

1   of us are going to argue that point, are we? *(Looks at RAFE.*

2   *RAFE looks stunned and nervous.)* **Good. Okay, Agent M is**

3   **hereby assigned Project Mass Exit.**

4   **RAFE: You win some, you lose some. What's next, Mike?**

5   **MIKE: This one's just a small operation, but no less significant.**

6   **We've got a reconnaissance team in need of a safe house.**

7   **Sherry, this looks like one for you.**

8   **SHERRY: All right! Time for the women to show you guys how it's**

9   **done!**

10   **MIKE: This is part of Operation Wall Fall. Who have you got in**

11   **place?**

12   **SHERRY:** *(Suddenly nervous)* **Um, did you say "Wall Fall"?**

13   **MIKE: Yes. Is there a problem?**

14   **SHERRY:** *(Recovering quickly)* **Problem? No, no. Of course not.**

15   **MIKE: So who's your agent?**

16   **SHERRY:** *(Looking in her folder, but concealing it from RAFE, who's*

17   *trying to look over her shoulder.)* **Oh, Agent R. Wonderful**

18   **woman. Very, um, professional.**

19   **GABE: Agent R? I'm not familiar with that one …**

20   **SHERRY: She's not from our usual pool of recruits.**

21   **RAFE: What's her background?**

22   **SHERRY: She's, um … an independent businesswoman.**

23   **RAFE: What sort of business?**

24   **SHERRY: She runs a house …** *(Covering quickly)*, **uh, a hotel.**

25   **RAFE:** *(Getting suspicious)* **She runs a house? What kind of house?**

26   **SHERRY: I said hotel! She runs a hotel!**

27   **GABE: You said house first.**

28   **MIKE: That's what I heard too.**

29   **SHERRY: OK! OK! It's Rahab! So she runs a bordello!**

30   **ALL:** *(Except SHERRY)* **A bordello?!**

31   **GABE: Forgive me, Sherry, but that's not exactly on the**

32   **Chairman's list of favorite occupations.**

33   **SHERRY: Look, I told you Rahab was from outside our regular**

34   **recruiting pool. She's not all that familiar with the**

35   **Chairman's policies yet.**

1 RAFE: Ignorance of the law is no excuse. Remember Agents A and E?
2 SHERRY: This has nothing to do with Project Serpent!
3 RAFE: Sounds to me like it has a lot to do with Project Serpent.
4 *(Jabs GABE in the elbow.)*
5 SHERRY: Cut it out, Rafe!
6 MIKE: Let me see her file, Sherry. *(She hands it to him. He looks at*
7 *it.)* Hmmm. Whoa! What's this? She's been tagged for Project
8 Redemption.
9 ALL: *(With astonishment)* **Redemption?!**
10 GABE: But that's years away!
11 MIKE: Nevertheless, apparently she's a key component for the
12 prep stage. With that kind of clearance, I'm not going to
13 object to her involvement in Wall Fall. You've got your safe
14 house, Sherry.
15 SHERRY: Thank you, sir.
16 RAFE: I have to admit, nobody's going to be looking for any of our
17 agents in a bordello.
18 MIKE: Zip it, Rafe.
19 RAFE: Just a joke, sir.
20 MIKE: Moving on, we're up for Project Slingshot.
21 RAFE: All right! I'll just turn that over to Agent S and it's all
22 wrapped up.
23 MIKE: Sorry, Rafe, but Agent S is persona non grata with the
24 Chairman right now.
25 RAFE: What? But he's got the assets in place! The man's got a ten
26 thousand-man army backing him up!
27 MIKE: According to our intel, that army isn't doing him much
28 good against Operation Goliath.
29 RAFE: This is King Saul we're talking about! He's been kicking
30 tail all over the region!
31 GABE: *(Looking in folder)* Not lately, he hasn't.
32 RAFE: So he's hit a little slump! Give him time!
33 MIKE: The Chairman says Agent S is out, so it's a moot point.
34 Who else have you got?
35 GABE: *(Looking in folder)* Agent D is available.

1 RAFE: The singer?
2 SHERRY: David? But he's just a kid!
3 GABE: *(Reading)* Says here he's a crack shot.
4 RAFE: So he can hit a tree with a rock! Mike, he's not ready for a
5   combat situation!
6 GABE: *(Still reading)* He's got tags for Project Kingdom, Project
7   Holy Writ and Project Redemption.
8 RAFE: Yeah, well what good is that gonna do him if you get him
9   killed?
10 MIKE: The Chairman's vouching for his safety. You can't get
11   better than that.
12 RAFE: It's the shepherd thing, isn't it? The Chairman's got this
13   thing for shepherds.
14 SHERRY: Relax, Rafe, he'll do fine.
15 MIKE: That's it. Agent D is our man.
16 RAFE: A musician. I can't believe we're sending in a musician. Next
17   thing we know, God will be using carpenters and fishermen.
18 MIKE: OK, that's it for today's assignments. Let's get started,
19   shall we? Put your wings on— and angels, let's be careful out
20   there.
21 RAFE: Great. We're stuck with Moses, Rahab and David. What
22   does God see in those losers?

Fourth and Ninety-nine

Synopsis: Robby "The Brick" Monroe is a member of the OMPFL: The One-Man Professional Football League. He plays every position on his team; in fact, he is the only team member! Needless to say, he has never won a game, nor is he likely to. But as he says, "There's nobody but me, so I get all the glory." The sketch reveals what can happen when we forget that God expects us to work together, not separately.

Theme: The Church is not a one-man endeavor.

Topics: Parts in the body of the church, spiritual gifts, teamwork

Type: Comedy

Cast: 2 men:
BARRY PRINCE — A talk show host
ROBBY MONROE — A football player
ROBBY'S MOTHER — A lady in the audience (No lines, just cheers.)

Props: Piece of paper

Set: Talk show type set: a desk for the host, sofa or two chairs for the guest, trash can by the host.

Sound Effect: Peppy talk show music

1   *(Both characters are seated when the sketch begins. ROBBY is*
2   *dressed in a generic football uniform. His arm is in a sling and*
3   *one leg is bandaged. Peppy talk show music plays.)*
4   **BARRY: Good morning, and welcome to *The Barry Prince Show.***
5   **We're here today with Robby "The Brick" Monroe, sole player**
6   **for the One-Man Professional Football League, or OMPFL.**
7   **ROBBY: Thanks for having me on the show, Barry.**
8   **BARRY: Glad to have you Robby. Now it says here you play for the**
9   **Pittsburgh Pirates.**
10   **ROBBY: Right you are, Barry.**
11   **BARRY: Robby, the Pirates are a baseball team.**
12   **ROBBY: Oh, I'm sorry, I don't play for the Pittsburgh Pirates.** *(He*
13   *emphasizes the "s.")* **It's Pirate— there's no "s."**
14   **BARRY: The Pittsburgh Pirate …**
15   **ROBBY: Yeah. Actually, it's the South Pittsburg Pirate, from South**
16   **Pittsburg, Tennessee.** *(To audience)* **Anybody here from South**
17   **Pittsburg?** *(ROBBY'S MOTHER stands up and cheers.)* **Other**
18   **than you, Ma!** *(To BARRY)* **Ma is great. She's such a fan.**
19   **BARRY: So Robby, what's it like to be a one-man football team?**
20   **ROBBY: It ain't easy, I can tell you that.**
21   **BARRY: What are some of your biggest challenges?**
22   **ROBBY: Well, I keep forgetting not to try a hand-off play.**
23   **BARRY: I can see where that wouldn't work.**
24   **ROBBY: Yeah. That's how this happened.** *(Indicates arm in sling.)*
25   **BARRY: Any other challenges?**
26   **ROBBY: Well, I've about got blocking figured out, but I'm still**
27   **having problems with the forward pass.**
28   **BARRY: So it's strictly a running game.**
29   **ROBBY: Well, I wouldn't say that either. Hey, I brought some stats,**
30   **to kind of give you a feel for how the game goes.** *(Hands a sheet*
31   *of paper to BARRY.)*
32   **BARRY: Let's have a look.** *(Reads.)* **Your average total forward**
33   **yardage per game is two hundred and ninety-three?! That's**
34   **pretty impressive.**
35   **ROBBY: Huh? Let me look at that.** *(Blows on paper to blow*

1   *something off.)* **Sorry, I had a powdered donut in the green**
2   **room. Some of it must have gotten on the sheet. Here.**
3 **BARRY: Ah, I see the minus sign now.**
4 **ROBBY: You know, maybe we really shouldn't go over those stats.**
5 **BARRY: That's not a bad suggestion.** *(Tosses sheet in trash can.)* **So,**
6   **Robby, since there's only the one team, who do you play?**
7 **ROBBY: Oh, all comers at this point. Although I have ruled out**
8   **peewee league teams now. It's just too dangerous.**
9 **BARRY: I can see you wouldn't want to hurt the kids.**
10 **ROBBY: Who's talking about the kids? It's too dangerous for me!**
11   **You don't know what it's like, eleven screaming eight-year-**
12   **olds charging toward you, each one of 'em knowing you're the**
13   **only thing standing between them and a McDonald's Happy**
14   **Meal.**
15 **BARRY: You don't have to tell me. I used to coach.** *(They both*
16   *shudder exaggeratedly.)* **Robby, don't you think you'd be**
17   **better off joining a full-size team?**
18 **ROBBY: What? Work with other people? Not for me, man. Other**
19   **people are just too difficult to deal with. Besides, this way I'm**
20   **the star. If you play for a team, the coach might stick you at**
21   **free safety or guard or center. Hey, I'm out there to shine.**
22   **There's nobody but me, so I get all the glory.**
23 **BARRY: Speaking of glory, what's your record like?**
24 **ROBBY: Sixty-seven and oh.**
25 **BARRY: Sixty-seven straight wins?**
26 **ROBBY: No, sixty-seven losses. Of course, since ties have been**
27   **eliminated, it makes my record seem worse than it is. You**
28   **can't get a feel for how close the games are just from the**
29   **record.**
30 **BARRY: OK, so how many overtime games have you had?**
31 **ROBBY: Well, none, actually. Most of my games are over before the**
32   **second half.**
33 **BARRY: You mean the other team gains such a big lead that you**
34   **can't make it up?**
35 **ROBBY: No, I mean most of my games are over because I'm being**

1   carried out on a stretcher. Oh, that reminds me. I'd like to say
2   a word of thanks to some folks back home. *(To "camera")* **Bob,**
3   **Jenny, Doctor Turner, thanks!**
4   **BARRY: Are they in the OMPFL?**
5   **ROBBY: No, they're in my HMO. I'm their number-one customer!**
6   *(To "camera")* **See ya again on Sunday afternoon!**
7   **BARRY: So, how many teams are in the OMPFL?**
8   **ROBBY: Well, only the one. But I'd like to take this moment to**
9   **announce an expansion, if I may.**
10 **BARRY: Go right ahead.**
11 **ROBBY: Thanks.** *(To "camera")* **Yo! Joey Falbrico in Schenectady!**
12   **Suit on up pal, it's cool with me. How about next October for**
13   **the first match-up? Call me, and we'll set it up.** *(To BARRY)*
14   **Joey's the Schenectady Screamer.**
15 **BARRY: Good name. He must be pretty fast.**
16 **ROBBY:** *(Not getting it)* **No, not really.** *(Brightens.)* **But he yells a**
17   **lot!** *(Beat)* **I think he does it to confuse his opponents.**
18 **BARRY: Does it work?**
19 **ROBBY: Sure confuses me!**
20 **BARRY: And what wouldn't?** *(Peppy music starts up. BARRY turns to*
21   *"camera.")* **Well, it sounds like that's all the time we have for**
22   **the show today. Thanks for joining us, and tune in next week**
23   **when our guest will be Harriet Willis, author of the new**
24   **bestseller *Women Are From Venus, but There's No Intelligent***
25   ***Life on Mars.*** *(Music continues.)*

Freeloader

Synopsis: When the husband's freeloading brother once again invades a couple's dinner time (asking for money for his latest crackpot business scheme), they try to encourage him to pursue a career — and stop mooching off of them. This comedy deals both with God's command that we work for a living and our need for a satisfying life's work instead of just a job.

Theme: How do we find work that we love?

Topics: Finding God's purpose for you, importance of work

Type: Comedy

Cast: 2 men, 1 woman:
JEFF — An accountant
JANICE — Jeff's wife
HARRY — Jeff's brother

Props: A checkbook, a decorative throw pillow, a tall decorative vase (or statue)

Set: JEFF and JANICE's living room. There is a table with a tall decorative vase (or statue) on it, a chair and a sofa. There is a pillow on the chair and a checkbook on the table.

Sound Effect: Doorbell

1   *(The sketch opens with JEFF in the living room. JEFF picks the*
2   *checkbook up from the table and hides it under the pillow. He sits*
3   *down just as JANICE enters.)*
4   **JEFF: Hi, honey, how was your day?**
5   **JANICE:** *(Flops down on the couch.)* **Same old, same old.**
6   **JEFF: Me too.** *(He tries to be nonchalant.)* **Oh, by the way, Harry's**
7   **coming over for dinner.**
8   **JANICE:** *(Sits up abruptly.)* **Again? Jeff, that's the eighth time this**
9   **month!**
10   **JEFF: Look, money's a little tight for Harry right now. The least**
11   **we can do is help him out with a meal from time to time.**
12   **JANICE : We've been "helping him out" for over two years!**
13   **JEFF: Now, Janice, you're exaggerating.**
14   **JANICE: I'm surprised you haven't asked him to move in.** *(JEFF*
15   *looks guilty.)* **You haven't.**
16   **JEFF: No, I haven't. I wouldn't do that without asking you first.**
17   **JANICE: Good.**
18   **JEFF: Besides, it would only be for a little while.**
19   **JANICE:** *(Stands up.)* **You'd better not be asking, because if you are**
20   **asking, let me just point out that no jury in this state would**
21   **convict me.**
22   **JEFF: I'm not asking, I'm not asking! Anyway, it may not even be**
23   **a consideration ...**
24   **JANICE: Let me reassure you, it's not.**
25   **JEFF: Harry told me he's finally got a business opportunity that**
26   **will put him over the top.**
27   **JANICE:** *(Looks around suspiciously.)* **OK. Where is it?**
28   **JEFF: Where's what?**
29   **JANICE: The checkbook. Hand it over.**
30   **JEFF: I don't have the checkbook. Why would I need the checkbook?**
31   **JANICE: Give it.**
32   **JEFF:** *(Reluctantly reaches under the pillow and hands JANICE the*
33   *checkbook.)* **Here.**
34   **JANICE:** *(Examines the book.)* **None missing. Good.**
35   **JEFF: Janice, I make investment decisions for my clients every**

1   day. I think you can trust me to make wise decisions with our
2   finances.
3 JANICE: I do. Except when it comes to Harry. *(Doorbell rings.)*
4 JEFF: There he is. Just try to be nice.
5 JANICE: Of course. You know me — Donna Reed all the way.
6   *(JEFF goes to open the door. JANICE picks up the vase and hefts*
7   *it like a club.)* No, we paid seventy dollars for this. I need
8   something cheaper. And heavier. *(JEFF and HARRY return as*
9   *JANICE puts down the vase.)*
10 HARRY: Janice! How good to see you!
11 JANICE: *(Brightly)* Harry! Go away!
12 HARRY: *(To JEFF)* Is this not a good time?
13 JEFF: No, it's fine, come on in. *(JANICE throws her hands up in*
14   *frustration as HARRY and JEFF sit down.)* Well, Harry, tell me
15   about this new business opportunity.
16 HARRY: You'll love this idea. It's a sure thing!
17 JANICE: A sure thing? Like the time you tried to sell carrier
18   pigeons as "nature's fax machine?"
19 HARRY: Hey, that could have worked. There was just too much
20   overhead involved.
21 JEFF: So what is this new idea?
22 HARRY: I call it the "Live-in Remote Control." It's a complete
23   entertainment package for today's busy family. I plan the
24   week's television viewing, tailored to each member: sports,
25   action and news for Dad; mini-series, romance and soaps for
26   Mom; and educational programming for the kids. All this plus
27   the added value of my scintillating wit and commentary to
28   enhance the family viewing experience.
29 JANICE: Great. He wants to be a professional couch potato.
30 HARRY: I prefer the term "home entertainment companion."
31 JEFF: I don't mean to discourage you, Harry, but I really don't see
32   a market for your, er, service.
33 HARRY: Well I don't want to live off you guys forever …
34 JANICE: Praise the Lord!
35 HARRY: I've got to find a way to bring in some money.

1   JANICE: Here's a novel idea, Harry: Get a job!

2   HARRY: Hey, I'd be happy to. But I'm just not cut out for that

3   whole "job" thing. I'm too independent ...

4   JANICE: That's a laugh.

5   HARRY: I'm vibrant, alive, carefree. I couldn't be tied down to

6   some boring nine-to-five routine like you guys.

7   JEFF: Oh, thank you.

8   HARRY: Hey, no offense. I just mean whatever I did would have to

9   be fun.

10   JEFF: *(Protesting)* My work is fun.

11   HARRY: Oh, come on, Jeff, who are you kidding? You're an

12   accountant. I fall asleep just thinking about it.

13   JEFF: Hey, I love accounting. To me it's like a big puzzle, making

14   each piece fit into the financial picture. It's challenging work,

15   and I love it.

16   HARRY: Yeah, and it brings in a nice chunk of change.

17   JEFF: We're doing OK, but the money's not the important thing,

18   Harry. That I love what I do is.

19   HARRY: So Janice, what do you love to do?

20   JANICE: Harry, right now you don't want to know what I'd love

21   to do.

22   JEFF: Look, Harry, you need to figure out what you enjoy, what

23   you have a talent for.

24   HARRY: *(Thinking it over.)* Hmmm. Well, I've always liked the sea ...

25   JANICE: Good. Be a sailor. *(She moves towards the "door" and*

26   *gestures out.)* The Navy recruiting office is downtown. Bye!

27   JEFF: Janice!

28   HARRY *(Still thinking)* ... and I like animals. I used to love "Flipper."

29   JEFF: There you go. Marine biology, oceanography, veterinary ...

30   JANICE: Waiter on a glass bottom boat.

31   HARRY: *(Brightening up — he's getting an idea.)* And I've always

32   been concerned with physical fitness.

33   JEFF: *(Not sure how this fits into the mix.)* Uh, ... scuba diver?

34   HARRY: *(Jumps up, excited.)* I've got it. I'll be a personal trainer

35   for fish!

1   **JEFF: What?**

2   **HARRY:** *(He heads for the door, talking excitedly to himself.)* **I'll**

3   **need a big aquarium, some waterproof barbells, maybe even**

4   **a tiny Nautilus machine ...** *(He exits.)*

5   **JEFF:** *(To JANICE)* **He's hopeless.**

6   **JANICE: I knew that.**

7   **HARRY:** *(Returns.)* **By the way, what's for dinner?**

8   **JANICE:** *(Mischievously)* **Fish!**

The Good Guys Club

Synopsis: Two friends want to apply for membership in the Good Guys Club but decide that their personal histories of failure mean that neither one will be acceptable. Rather than ask for the membership requirements, they leave to "do good" in hopes that this will earn them admittance later. (See the alternate version, "Joe and Lou.")

Theme: What is required to enter heaven?

Topics: Earning salvation, faith vs. works, grace, imperfection, sin

Type: Comedy

Cast: 2 men:
MIKE — A member wannabe
SAM — A member wannabe

Props: None

Set: A door, placed at Center Stage so it faces the audience. A large sign on the door reads, "The Good Guys Club. Applicants Welcome."

1 *(SAM stands to the side of the door. As MIKE enters, SAM looks*
2 *at the door, starts to approach it, shakes his head, and backs away*
3 *nervously.)*
4 MIKE: *(Sees SAM.)* Sam! Is that you? Good to see you, buddy!
5 SAM: Hi, Mike. What are you doing here?
6 MIKE: I'm here to join the Good Guys Club. Are you headed in
7   too?
8 SAM: I was, but now I'm not so sure.
9 MIKE: Why not? Don't you want to join?
10 SAM: Sure I do. I … I just don't think they'll take me.
11 MIKE: What are you talking about? Why wouldn't they take you?
12 SAM: Because I'm not really a good guy. And I'm certainly not
13   good enough to be in the Good Guys Club.
14 MIKE: Oh come on, Sam. You're a great guy. Didn't you tell me
15   just last week that you bought lunch for a homeless man?
16 SAM: Well, that's not really what happened. Truth is, I was eating
17   lunch in the park, and when this guy got near me, I freaked
18   and threw my Big Mac at him and ran away.
19 MIKE: *(Looking for a bright spot)* But he did get a meal out of it.
20 SAM: I'm not even sure he was homeless. He might have just been
21   a grad student.
22 MIKE: Yeah, who can tell? But at least your heart was in the right
23   place.
24 SAM: You mean in my throat? No, I've got to face it: I'm just not
25   a good guy.
26 MIKE: Look, Sam. I know you, and I know you're not a bad guy.
27 SAM: Oh, yes I am. I'm a rotten guy.
28 MIKE: What are you talking about? You've never done anything
29   bad.
30 SAM: No? Do you remember Melinda?
31 MIKE: Of course I do. Nice girl. Whatever happened between you
32   guys?
33 SAM: A lot that shouldn't have, that's what. I made some bad
34   decisions, and now I just have to take the consequences. One
35   of which is that I can't get in there. *(Indicates the club.)*

1   MIKE: I can't believe they would blackball you just because of
2   Melinda. That was years ago!
3   SAM: Does that matter? That's the Good Guys Club! They have
4   standards to maintain. Anyway, it's not just Melinda. It's
5   hundreds of things, thousands of things I've done, all wrong,
6   all bad enough to keep me out of the Good Guys Club.
7   MIKE: There must be something you can do about that.
8   SAM: Believe me, I've tried. I've done volunteer work, led charity
9   drives, smiled at old people. I've even picked up stray kittens.
10   I have the rabies shots to prove it.
11   MIKE: But that's all terrific! You're a shoe-in.
12   SAM: But it doesn't matter, Mike. It all goes wrong. When I
13   delivered meals to shut-ins I got so obsessed with getting the
14   food there while it was still hot that I ran stop signs, cut off
15   school buses, cussed out elderly drivers — I even ran a pizza
16   delivery guy off the road.
17   MIKE: So you're from Nashville. *(Use the name of your town instead*
18   *of "Nashville.")* Who's gonna notice?
19   SAM: I'm glad you can laugh about it. It's not like you're going to
20   get in or anything.
21   MIKE: Whoa there! Who says I'm not going to get in?
22   SAM: Yeah, right! Mike, if I can't get in there, they're certainly not
23   going to take you. No offense.
24   MIKE: I'll have you know, I'm a terrific guy. I'll sail through those
25   doors with ease.
26   SAM: Sure you will. On your way out.
27   MIKE: Oh, really. And what makes you think I won't get into the
28   club?
29   SAM: Three little letters: I-R-S. *(MIKE looks visibly startled.)* You
30   may not remember, buddy, but you told me all about your
31   little tax preparation techniques.
32   MIKE: I just claim what I'm entitled to.
33   SAM: Really? And who else claims dependents named "Rover"
34   and "Fluffy"?
35   MIKE: Hey, they're part of the family.

1 SAM: What about your deductions for donations to the "Church of
2   High Living"?
3 MIKE: The luxuries of life are an article of faith with me. Besides,
4   it's the IRS. Who cares if I bend the tax rules a little?
5 SAM: They do. *(Indicates the Good Guys Club.)*
6 MIKE: *(Thinks about it.)* Yeah, they would, wouldn't they?
7 SAM: You bet they would. And if they'll hold that against you,
8   imagine all the other stuff you've done that they'll be waiting
9   to slam you with.
10 MIKE: *(Thinking about it)* Yeah … *(Suddenly looks worried. He's*
11   *thought of something worse.)* Yeah! *(With realization.)* Oh man,
12   I'm not going to get in.
13 SAM: See, I told you. No way am I walking through that door.
14 MIKE: Do you think they might make an exception?
15 SAM: No. But if you want to find out, go right ahead.
16 MIKE: *(Starts toward door, stops.)* Forget it.
17 SAM: Smart move.
18 MIKE: *(Brightens.)* I've got it!
19 SAM: What?
20 MIKE: We'll team up. We'll go in together, back each other up. If we
21   put up a united front, we might get through. It's worth a shot.
22 SAM: Not a bad idea. Let's try it. *(They stand together briefly and*
23   *look at the door.)*
24 MIKE: So, want to see if that homeless guy needs some French
25   fries?
26 SAM: Deal. *(They leave, walking away from the door. Lights, if*
27   *available, remain on the door, then blackout.)*

Joe and Lou
(The Good Guys Club 2)

Synopsis: Joe wants to enter the Good Guys Club, but Lou (Lucifer), a "former member," convinces Joe that he doesn't have what it takes to be admitted. In the end, Joe decides to join Lou's club, which promises that Joe will "never have to live up to anything at all." The sketch looks at how the Devil deceives us about God's real expectations. (See the alternate version, "The Good Guys Club.")

Theme: What is required to enter heaven?

Topics: Faith vs. works, grace, sin, earning salvation, imperfection, guilt, the Devil

Type: Comedy/Drama

Cast: 2 men:
JOE — A member wannabe
LOU — A former member

Props: None

Set: A door, placed at Center Stage so it faces the audience. A large sign on the door reads, "The Good Guys Club. Applicants welcome."

1   *(LOU lounges to the side, near the door. JOE enters.)*

2   **JOE:** *(To audience)* **See that door over there? That's the entrance to**

3   **the Good Guys Club. I've heard about it all my life. It's**

4   **supposed to be the most fabulous place: food like you wouldn't**

5   **believe, luxuries you couldn't begin to imagine, nonstop fun**

6   **and excitement. Everybody who's anybody is supposed to be**

7   **there. And that's where I'm going. I'm going to walk right in**

8   **and ask for a membership.** *(He walks over to the door.)*

9   **LOU:** *(Stepping forward, and incidentally blocking the entrance)*

10   **Hello there, friend! Where are you headed this fine day?**

11   **JOE: What? Oh, I'm going to the Good Guys Club.**

12   **LOU: I thought you looked like the type. When I saw you walking**

13   **up, I said to myself, now there's a member of the Good Guys**

14   **Club if I've ever seen one.**

15   **JOE: Oh, but I'm not a member. Not yet, anyway.**

16   **LOU:** *(With dismay)* **Not a member? But how do you expect to get in?**

17   **JOE: Well, I thought I'd just ask for an application …**

18   **LOU:** *(Laughs in knowing way.)* **Oh, come now, young … what did**

19   **you say your name was?**

20   **JOE: Joe.**

21   **LOU: Look, young Joe, surely you don't think it's as easy to get in**

22   **as all that, do you?**

23   **JOE: Well, I really didn't think —**

24   **LOU:** *(Interrupting)* **Of course you didn't. Why, the Good Guys**

25   **Club is a very exclusive organization. I should know. I was**

26   **once a member in good standing myself.**

27   **JOE: You were a member? But why aren't you now?**

28   **LOU: Oh, I had a minor disagreement with the leadership**

29   **structure, so I resigned my membership on my own**

30   **recognizance.** *(This last line confuses JOE. He is obviously*

31   *trying to decipher what it means, but LOU continues unabated.)*

32   **But I assure you the club's membership concerns are**

33   **intertwined very tightly with my own.**

34   **JOE:** *(Brightening)* **So you must know all about the membership**

35   **requirements!**

1   LOU: Every jot and tittle, so to speak.

2   JOE: Do you suppose you could tell me how it all works?

3   LOU: Why, my young friend, I'd like nothing better than to give

4   you all the advice I can muster. Steering the unfortunates who

5   come my way is all I live for.

6   JOE: *(Suspicious)* So how much is this advice going to cost?

7   LOU: Why, it won't cost me a thing! *(Laughs at his joke. JOE is not*

8   *sure whether to be amused or not.)* Seriously, you won't have to

9   pay me anything ... and besides, why worry about cost when

10   blissful happiness is your goal?

11   JOE: That's true.

12   LOU: Now, first of all, Joe, you probably consider yourself a pretty

13   good guy, am I right?

14   JOE: Well, yes, as a matter of fact, I do. That's why I want to apply

15   for a membership.

16   LOU: Of course it is. But since, as you say, you are already a good

17   guy, do you really *need* a membership in some club to confirm

18   it?

19   JOE: Well ...

20   LOU: Of course you don't. You already know. So why not just go

21   on enjoying your life without all the hassles that a

22   membership would surely entail? Doesn't that sound like the

23   best choice?

24   JOE: I can see that it might ... but no, no. I really do want a

25   membership.

26   LOU: A wise choice indeed, young Joe. You must understand that

27   my initial question was merely designed to ascertain whether

28   or not you are truly fit material for the Good Guys Club. After

29   all, my loyalties to the club haven't changed from the moment

30   I left. It wouldn't do for me to send any riffraff through that

31   door.

32   JOE: No, of course not.

33   LOU: And your determination clearly shows that you are not the

34   riffraff sort. No, you are truly a fine example of a human

35   being ... but are you, Joe, really a Good Guy?

1   JOE: Well, yeah. I mean, I'm not a murderer or anything like that.

2   LOU: No, few people are. But does that really matter to the Good

3   Guys?

4   JOE: I would think it does, wouldn't you?

5   LOU: To be sure, to be sure. But the question really isn't what you

6   are, is it? It's what you aren't, wouldn't you say?

7   JOE: I'm not sure what you mean.

8   LOU: *(Grabs JOE and gestures towards the door.)* Look at it, Joe.

9   That's the Good Guys Club! Do you think they are going to let

10   anybody who isn't good into that club?

11   JOE: Well, of course not …

12   LOU: And do you think they are going to let anybody who is bad

13   into that club?

14   JOE: Certainly not.

15   LOU: Well, Joe, are you good enough for that?

16   JOE: Well, I don't …

17   LOU: Joe, I'm going to tell you something that will open your eyes.

18   They have a list in that club — actually they have two lists.

19   And on those lists are every good thing and bad thing you've

20   ever done.

21   JOE: Everything?

22   LOU: All of it.

23   JOE: That's kind of scary.

24   LOU: It's frightening, Joe. And they check those lists with intense

25   scrutiny. Tell me, Joe, what do you think will happen to an

26   applicant who has more on his Badness List than his

27   Goodness List?

28   JOE: They'd probably kick him out the door.

29   LOU: Of course! What else would you expect from the Good Guys

30   Club? Now, Joe, what about your lists? I know you think

31   you're a good guy, but are you really more of a good guy than

32   a bad one?

33   JOE: I … I don't know.

34   LOU: Well, ask yourself this: Do you really think you've done

35   enough good to outweigh the bad? And before you answer, let

1   me tell you they weigh the bad pretty heavily in there.

2   JOE: Well, I ...

3   LOU: Let me put it this way: Do you think that you, Joe, with all

4   the rotten things you've done in your life — and we both know

5   what I'm talking about — do you think you can walk in there

6   and not face any consequences? How do you really think

7   they're going to react to a request for an application from,

8   let's face it, a moral degenerate such as yourself?

9   JOE: They'll kick me out before I get in the door.

10   LOU: Joe, I commend you. Too many people never realize the peril

11   they place themselves in when they walk through that door.

12   You, however, are a man who knows your true character.

13   JOE: *(Dejected)* Yes. Yes, I do.

14   LOU: Now Joe, having recognized this, do you really think you're

15   worthy of a membership in the Good Guys Club?

16   JOE: No.

17   LOU: Joe, you are a man of unparalleled wisdom. And I think

18   you're wise enough to see that the Good Guys Club is not for

19   you. But you are in luck. You see, I have a club you are

20   welcome to join without restriction. *(He begins to lead JOE*

21   *away from the door.)*

22   JOE: You do?

23   LOU: Yes. And in my club, you never have to worry about rules and

24   restrictions or keeping up with any Goodness List. In fact, you

25   never have to live up to anything at all. How does that sound?

26   JOE: I guess that's where I belong. I'm glad I met you; you've

27   really straightened me out, uh, uh ... say, you never told me

28   your name.

29   LOU: Oh? Well, it's out of fashion these days. But you can call me

30   Lou. *(They exit.)*

The List of Life

Synopsis: Following a suggestion from a self-help book, a woman makes a list of her life goals and achievements, only to decide that they have little value to her. She longs for a deeper sense of purpose but doesn't know where to turn. Her boyfriend makes suggestions, but even he doesn't seem to understand her feelings. In the end she wonders if there is anyone who can help her find meaning in her life.

Theme: Where do we turn for true fulfillment in life?

Topics: Finding God's purpose, fulfillment, our need for God, relationship with God

Type: Drama

Cast: 1 man, 1 woman:
JEN — A young woman, thirties
BILL — Jen's boyfriend

Props: Phone, pencil, notepad, book

Set: Jen's apartment. We see a sofa and coffee table. A phone sits on the table.

**Sound
Effect:** Doorbell

1   *(JEN sits at the sofa, writing on a notepad. A large book is beside*
2   *her on the sofa.)*
3 JEN: OK, let's see. Graduate from college: check. With honors:
4   also check. Get a job: check. Get a great job: Well, there's a
5   steady paycheck, so ... partial check.
6   Make more than 50k a year before my fortieth birthday:
7   working on it.
8   Find a nice guy: Yeah, lot's of 'em. And they're all married.
9   Find an acceptable guy: Does Bill count? I'll put a dash down.
10   Get married, settle down, have kids, own a house with a
11   white picket fence, two cats and a shaggy dog of uncertain
12   pedigree: The way things are going with Bill, apparently not
13   in this lifetime.
14   Have a body like Cindy Crawford: Yeah. Right.
15   Just stay healthy and be content with the body I have:
16   That's doable.
17   Be reasonably well informed on issues of politics, the arts
18   and economics: Hmmm. I saw *Primary Colors*, so we'll make
19   that a check.
20   Well, that's the list of my life. Boy, when you put it down on
21   paper, it doesn't look like much. OK, what's next? *(Picks up book*
22   *and reads.)* "Study your list carefully. On a separate piece of
23   paper, write a short paragraph about each item you have
24   checked off as complete. Describe how achieving each goal
25   makes you feel." Hmmm. Right now, not much at all. That's the
26   whole reason I'm doing this. Stupid book. *(She puts the book*
27   *down and continues to talk to it.)* So far none of those things have
28   gotten me anywhere. I'm glad I've done them, I guess, but right
29   now I just don't feel like they mean anything at all.
30   What am I doing? I'm talking to a book. Maybe Susan could
31   help me sort this out. *(Picks up phone, dials, waits for answer.)*
32   Hey, it's me. *(Pause)* Nothing much, really. That's sort of the
33   problem. *(Pause)* That's just it, I don't know what's wrong. I just
34   don't seem to feel anything. *(Pause)* Am I down? Well, I'm
35   certainly not up. I don't really know if I'm down or not — like I

1 said, I just don't seem to feel much of anything. *(Pause)* No, it's
2 not Bill. At least I don't think it is. We have a great time together.
3 *(Pause)* I don't know. I'm just wondering if this is all there is. Is
4 the rest of my life just going to be more of the same? *(Pause)*
5 What? *(Picks up book and reads cover.)* **Putting Your Life in**
6 **Perfect Perspective.** Yeah, I know it. I've got it right here. And so
7 far the perspective it's given me is pretty puny. *(Pause)* Yeah,
8 everybody says it helps, but I can't seem to get anything out of
9 it. This book makes my life seem like a series of hoops to jump
10 through. I don't see any purpose in that. What was that? *(Pause)*
11 Susan, it sounds like Jeremy needs you. You don't have to hang
12 on with me. *(Pause)* No really, it's all right. You've got your
13 hands full. We can talk later. *(Pause)* I'll be fine. Take care.
14 *(Hangs up. Sighs. Looks at book cover.)* **Putting Your Life in Perfect**
15 **Perspective**? OK, here's my perspective: Nothing seems to
16 matter, nothing seems to mean anything. How's that? *(Doorbell*
17 *rings twice rapidly. JEN calls out.)* Come on in, Bill. It's open.
18 BILL: *(Enters.)* Jen, you really shouldn't leave your door unlocked.
19 I could have been anybody.
20 JEN: *(Without emotion)* Hi, Bill.
21 BILL: Well, that's not the greeting I expected.
22 JEN: I'm sorry, Bill. I haven't been in the best mood lately.
23 BILL: So I've noticed. What's bugging you?
24 JEN: It's hard for me to say. I don't seem to be connecting with
25 anything.
26 BILL: That's nice and vague. Is there anything specific you mean?
27 JEN: It's everything, Bill. I don't feel particularly good about
28 anything.
29 BILL: Well, just kick a big chunk out of my self-esteem.
30 JEN: I don't mean you, Bill.
31 BILL: No, wait. What do you feel about me?
32 JEN: I'm not sure, Bill. I like you a lot, and I enjoy being with you.
33 But I haven't known you long enough yet to go beyond that.
34 Please believe me when I say this isn't about you.
35 BILL: OK, I guess I'll have to accept that. So what is it about?

1   JEN: I can't seem to find a point to anything. I feel like I'm going
2   through the motions of life, but there isn't any reason for what
3   I'm doing.
4   BILL: Maybe you need to do one of those self-assessment things.
5   There's this book I've heard about … *(JEN holds up the book)*
6   and that would be it. I gather it's not helping.
7   JEN: There's nothing wrong with the book, but it's not what I need.
8   When I look at my life through the eyes of that book, I don't see
9   anything there. All my goals, all my accomplishments, they just
10   seem kind of flat.
11 BILL: Flat?
12 JEN: Artificial, arbitrary, pointless. Take your pick.
13 BILL: Maybe you should talk to a counselor.
14 JEN: Oh, come on, Bill. What kind of answer is that?
15 BILL: A good one.
16 JEN: No, it's a pat one. Whenever anybody doesn't understand a
17   problem or can't answer a question or wants to end an
18   uncomfortable conversation, they suggest the other person
19   "seek counseling."
20 BILL: What's wrong with counseling?
21 JEN: Nothing's wrong with it. I just don't know that counseling is
22   what I need.
23 BILL: But if you're feeling depressed …
24 JEN: I'm not feeling depressed. That's not what I'm feeling at all.
25 BILL: So what are you feeling?
26 JEN: *(Takes a short, deep breath.)* OK, you want to know what I'm
27   feeling? I'm feeling nothing. I'm looking at my life and I don't
28   see any meaning in it. I don't see any point to the past, and I
29   don't see any purpose for my future. Everything I've done and
30   everything I hope to do are nothing but check marks on a
31   page — like I'm doing things just to mark time, just to say
32   I've done them. I don't have any reason for any of it, and right
33   now I don't feel anything about any of it. I don't feel any
34   highs, I don't feel any lows. Nothing. That's what I'm feeling.
35   Now, who can I talk to about that? *(Freeze and blackout.)*

The Loser Olympics

Synopsis: Three contestants in the Loser Olympics vie for the title of "World's Greatest Loser." The final round is the 100-meter dash, yet before it starts, each contestant offers a unique excuse for forfeiting the race. One believes the officials are against him, one is afraid of failure and the last is just too lazy to try.

Theme: Why do we expect the worst of ourselves?

Topics: Being a winner, fear of failure, losing, negative/positive attitude, self-esteem, self-worth, success, talents

Type: Comedy

Cast: 4 men (or 3 men and 1 woman), 3–5 non speaking roles, 3–5 minor Off-stage parts:
ANNOUNCER — Host for the Olympics. Cheesy, Don Pardo type.
DON DOWNS — The Ultimate Whiner
BUDDY KANT — The Quintessential Quitter
(or BETTY KANT — The Queen of Quitters)
MILTON SLOTH — The King of the Couch Potatoes
FOUR JUDGES — Non-speaking; excellent for youth or children
CHEERING SECTION — Three or more people in the audience.
MOUSEKETEER — Non-speaking. A child wearing a Mickey Mouse hat.

Performance Notes: The Announcer should be as cheesy as possible. He's "in on the joke," so even when he interacts with the contestants, he speaks in a backstage announcer-type voice, flashes his best "on-camera" grin, etc.

Props: Folding lawnchair; bag of potato chips; remote control; three signs for each judge reading "Weenie," "Wimp" and "Total Loser"; note card; play money

Set: The field of an athletic event. Place four chairs at the rear of the stage.

**Sound
Effect:** Olympic fanfare music

1   *(The four JUDGES sit in chairs near the back of the stage.*
2   *MILTON holds the folded lawn chair, the bag of potato chips, and*
3   *the remote control. BUDDY is jogging in place excitedly. DON*
4   *stands with his hands in his pockets, looking suspiciously at*
5   *everyone. The ANNOUNCER stands at Center Stage, facing the*
6   *audience. Olympic fanfare plays.)*
7   **ANNOUNCER:** *(To audience)* **Welcome back to the Loser**
8   **Olympics. We're down to our final three contenders in the**
9   **Loser's Decathlon, all struggling for the title of World's**
10   **Greatest Loser. To my left we have Milton Sloth, known to**
11   **fans around the world as the King of the Couch Potatoes ...**
12   *(MILTON waves.)* **Buddy Kant, the Quintessential Quitter ...**
13   **BUDDY:** *(Excited, perky)* **Oh, this is so exciting!**
14   **DON:** *(Glaring at BUDDY)* **No, it's not.**
15   **BUDDY:** *(Completely defeated, he stops jogging.)* **Oh. You're right.**
16   **It's not.**
17   **ANNOUNCER: ... and Don Downs, the Ultimate Whiner.**
18   **DON: This game's probably rigged.**
19   **ANNOUNCER: Our final competition is the 100-meter dashed**
20   **hopes. Don, you're our first contestant today.**
21   **DON:** *(Complaining)* **Oh, man. I knew I'd have to go first.**
22   **ANNOUNCER: On your mark ... get set ... go!**
23   **DON:** *(Stands up suddenly and points at the announcer.)* **You did that**
24   **on purpose!**
25   **ANNOUNCER:** *(Surprised.)* **Did what?**
26   **DON: You said "go" before I was ready.**
27   **ANNOUNCER: I gave you plenty of time to get ready.**
28   **DON: Oh, sure. I know you don't want me to win. If nobody's**
29   **going to let me win, I just won't even play.**
30   **ANNOUNCER: Judges? Your decisions?** *(The JUDGES hold up*
31   *signs: "Total Loser," "Total Loser," "Total Loser," "Weenie.")*
32   **I'm sorry, Don. You've got three total losers, but apparently**
33   **the Brazilian judge thinks you're a weenie.** *(One of the*
34   *JUDGES rudely sticks out her tongue at DON.)*
35   **DON: I could tell she didn't like me when I first saw her. I told you**

1   **this whole thing was rigged.** *(Exits.)*

2   **ANNOUNCER: Our next contestant is Buddy Kant. Buddy?**

3   **BUDDY:** *(Excited)* **I'm so ready for this.**

4   **DON:** *(From Off-stage)* **No, you're not.** *(BUDDY is shaken by this, but*

5   *steps up to the line.)*

6   **ANNOUNCER: On your mark ... get set ... go!** *(BUDDY starts to*

7   *run, but immediately the CHEERING SECTION stands up and*

8   *begins shouting.)*

9   **CHEERING SECTION: Go Buddy, go! Go Buddy, go!** *(They*

10   *continue chanting throughout. BUDDY stops abruptly.)*

11   **ANNOUNCER: Is there a problem?**

12   **BUDDY:** *(Timidly)* **Who are they?**

13   **ANNOUNCER: I'd say those people are your fans.**

14   **BUDDY:** *(Alarmed)* **You mean they're cheering for me?**

15   **ANNOUNCER: Surprising as that may seem, yes.**

16   **BUDDY: They're expecting me to win?**

17   **ANNOUNCER: Yes.**

18   **BUDDY:** *(Horrified)* **I can't take that kind of pressure!**

19   **ANNOUNCER: What?**

20   **BUDDY:** *(He hides behind the ANNOUNCER.)* **Make them stop!**

21   **ANNOUNCER:** *(He motions to the CHEERING SECTION to be quiet.*

22   *They stop chanting.)* **Judges?** *(The JUDGES hold up their signs:*

23   *"Weenie," "Wimp," "Wimp," "Total Loser.")* **A weenie, two wimps**

24   **and a total loser. I'm sorry Buddy, that's impressive, but not**

25   **enough for the title.**

26   **BUDDY:** *(Dejected)* **See? I knew I couldn't win.** *(Exits.)*

27   **ANNOUNCER: Next we have Milton Sloth. Milton?**

28   **MILTON:** *(Steps up to the line.)* **Yo! Right here!**

29   **ANNOUNCER: Are you ready?**

30   **MILTON: I'm ready.**

31   **ANNOUNCER: On your mark ... get set ... go!** *(MILTON unfolds*

32   *the lawn chair, sits down, points the remote as if at a TV set, and*

33   *starts eating potato chips.)* **What are you doing?**

34   **MILTON: I'm watching the 100-meters. Is it on NBC?**

35   **ANNOUNCER: You're not supposed to watch it, you're supposed**

1   **to run it!**
2   **MILTON:** *(Shocked)* **Me?**
3   **ANNOUNCER: Yes, you.**
4   **MILTON: I don't know. A hundred meters is pretty far, isn't it?**
5   **ANNOUNCER: How should I know? I'm an American.**
6   **MILTON: Couldn't I just drive it?**
7   **ANNOUNCER: I think you're really supposed to run it.**
8   **MILTON: Run? Ooh, no thanks. Maybe it's on cable.**
9   **ANNOUNCER: Judges, your totals please?** *(The JUDGES hold up*
10   *signs: "Total Loser," "Total Loser," "Total Loser," "Total*
11   *Loser.")* **Congratulations, Milton Sloth. You are the World's**
12   **Greatest Loser!**
13   **MILTON:** *(Stands up excitedly, pointing towards the imaginary TV*
14   *set.)* **Hey! Whatta ya know?! I won!**
15   **ANNOUNCER: What are you going to do next?** *(A MOUSEKETEER*
16   *runs out and hands MILTON a note card and a large handful of play*
17   *money, then runs back Off-stage.)*
18   **MILTON:** *(Reads card.)* **"I'm going to Disneyland." Gee, that's**
19   **pretty far. How about if I just watch the Disney Channel**
20   **instead?**

The Main Event

Synopsis: It's a knock-down, drag-out, no-holds-barred fight to the finish — and it's happening in the family room. Jane and John Smith are at it again, slamming each other with insults and accusations, all over a visit from the mother-in-law. Set up as a full-fledged prize fight (with announcer and ringside seating for the kids), this farce packs a wallop about the importance of loving and respecting each other — even when we disagree.

Theme: Why do we let the simplest disagreements turn into big arguments?

Topics: Arguments, communication, family fights, marital problems, marriage, relationships, respect

Type: Comedy

Cast: 3 men, 2 women, 1 boy, 1 girl:

JANE SMITH — A wife and mother who wears gym shorts, a T-shirt, white socks and sneakers. She also wears a robe.

JOHN SMITH — A husband and father who is dressed like his wife.

JIMMY SMITH — Their son, about age ten

JENNY SMITH — Their daughter, about age twelve

ANNOUNCER — Wrestling/fight announcer. Can be On-stage or an Off-stage voice.

GERALDINE JONES — Jane's mother and coach

BUDDY BROWN — John's golfing buddy and coach. Divorced.

Props: A sofa, three posts (that are three- to four-feet high) with hooks for ropes, two six-foot ropes for the posts, three cheap lamp shades, two game control pads, a newspaper, a book, a large tub of popcorn, two towels, two water bottles (squirt kind), two small "spit" buckets, golf bag with a few clubs.

Set: The Smith family den. There is a sofa and three "lamp stands" (actually the three posts with lamp shades on them) On-stage. One of the lamps is Stage Left of the sofa, the other two are located Downstage Center to the left and right, about ten to twelve feet apart.

**Sound
Effect:** Drum roll, bell

1   *(JIMMY and JENNY are on the floor, Downstage Center between*

2   *the "lamps," "playing" a video game [the screen is located in the*

3   *audience]. JOHN sits on the couch in a robe, reading a newspaper.*

4   *JANE, who also wears a robe, sits next to him, reading a book. The*

5   *dialog starts sweetly, but builds to fighting level.)*

6   **JANE:** John, dear …

7   **JOHN:** *(Sweetly, but without putting down paper)* **Yes, Jane?**

8   **JANE:** Did you remember this is the weekend my mother is coming

9   to visit?

10   **JOHN:** I'm sorry, dear, but this weekend is my big golfing day with

11   Buddy.

12   **JANE:** Now, John, I told you my mother would be coming at least

13   three weeks ago.

14   **JOHN:** No, sweetheart, you told me your mother *might* be coming.

15   **JANE:** So you scheduled a golfing day after I told you?

16   **JOHN:** Jane, you know Buddy and I play golf once a month.

17   **JANE:** You played golf two weeks ago!

18   **JOHN:** Right. That was last month, this is this month.

19   **JANE:** *(Angry)* You always schedule a golf day when my mother

20   comes to visit!

21   **JOHN:** *(Angry)* Well, you always invite your mother when you

22   know I'm going to play golf!

23   **JIMMY and JENNY:** *(To each other, excitedly)* **Fight!** *(Drum roll*

24   *starts. JOHN and JANE jump out of the sofa, throwing off their*

25   *robes. They are wearing gym shorts, T-shirts, sneakers, and white*

26   *socks. They get into a fighting stance. JIMMY and JENNY push*

27   *the couch back and pull a big tub of popcorn and the ropes from*

28   *behind the couch. They create a boxing ring out of the "lamp*

29   *stands," behind JOHN and JANE. BUDDY and GERALDINE*

30   *enter Stage Right and Left, carrying water bottles and towels.*

31   *BUDDY also carries his golf bag.)*

32   **ANNOUNCER:** *(Off-stage, over drum roll)* **Ladies and gentlemen,**

33   **sixteen twenty-three Haywood Lane is proud to present the**

34   **Main Event! In the left corner, weighing in at one hundred**

35   **and seventy-two pounds …**

1   JANE: *(To JOHN)* Ha! You wish!
2   ANNOUNCER: ... the Sultan of Suburbia, John "Everyman" Smith!
3   JANE: Boooo!
4   ANNOUNCER: And in the right corner, weighing in at ...
5   JANE: *(To the voice)* Hey! Watch it!
6   ANNOUNCER: *(A little intimidated)* ... an undisclosed amount, the
7   Queen of the Kitchen, Jane "Soccer Mom" Smith! *(JOHN*
8   *mimes 1-3-7 with his hands to the audience during the "weight"*
9   *dialog.)* Ladies and Gentlemen, are you ready to rumble?!
10   *(During the "fight," JOHN and JANE mime punches or react as*
11   *if hit with each insult. It should be visibly clear to the audience*
12   *that the punches come nowhere near the other person; the "hit"*
13   *is from the words, not the action.)*
14   JOHN: *(To audience)* She better be, 'cause I'm gonna take her out
15   in two!
16   GERALDINE: Ha! You can't even take out the garbage!
17   JOHN: Oh, yeah? We took you out to dinner last month, didn't
18   we?
19   JANE: Leave my mother out of this!
20   JOHN: Believe me, I'd love to, but her nose keeps getting in the
21   way! *(A bell rings.)*
22   ANNOUNCER: And that's the first round!
23   JENNY: *(To JIMMY)* I'll bet you two Pokemon cards that Mom
24   takes him before the third round.
25   JIMMY: You're on! *(JANE and JOHN begin to weave around each*
26   *other.)*
27   BUDDY: Watch your left, watch your left!
28   JANE: I can't believe you care more about some old golf game
29   than my mother!
30   JOHN: *(Unfazed)* Babe, I care more about my golf *socks* than I do
31   your mother! *(JANE staggers as if punched.)*
32   BUDDY: Oooo, way to whack her, John!
33   JANE: You weren't like this when we dated!
34   JOHN: I didn't know your mother when we dated! *(Bell rings*
35   *again. JANE and JOHN retreat to their corners. JANE looks*

1   *harried, but JOHN is upbeat and confident.)*

2   **BUDDY: John, you are really letting her have it!**

3   **JOHN: You don't think I'm being too hard on her?**

4   **BUDDY: You wanna play golf this weekend? You've got to lay**

5   **down the law! That's what I did with my ex!** *(JOHN looks at*

6   *him with some doubt.)*

7   **GERALDINE: Come here, dear.** *(Hugs JANE, pats her back.)* **Now**

8   **listen, Janie, you're swinging wild. You've got to hit him where**

9   **it counts. Try the Bobby Latham maneuver.** *(JANE brightens.*

10   *Bell sounds. JANE and JOHN move to center again.)*

11   **JANE: Speaking of golf, I ran into one of your old teammates from**

12   **school yesterday.**

13   **JOHN:** *(Surprised at her change, suspicious, lowering hands.)* **Yeah?**

14   **BUDDY: John! Don't let your guard down!**

15   **JANE: You remember Robert Latham, don't you?**

16   **JOHN:** *(Wounded, but standing)* **Yeah. I remember.**

17   **JANE: Oh, that's right. I forgot you knew Bobby and I ...** *dated.*

18   *(JOHN reacts with a head snap, as if hit from the left.)*

19   **BUDDY: Ow!**

20   **JANE:** *(Continuing)* **Did you know he's a** *doctor* **now?** *(JOHN snaps*

21   *head the opposite way.)*

22   **BUDDY: Oooo!**

23   **JANE:** *(Continuing)* **I was thinking of recommending him to Mom.**

24   **She always liked him.** *(JOHN reacts to gut punch.)*

25   **BUDDY: Oh! That's gotta hurt!**

26   **JANE:** *(Continuing)* **You know, he never married. I wonder why?**

27   *(JOHN snaps head back. She zeroes in.)* **I asked him about golf.**

28   **He says he's a scratch handicap now. That's pretty good, isn't**

29   **it?** *(JOHN staggers back to ropes.)*

30   **BUDDY: What's the matter with you?! I saw that coming a mile**

31   **off!**

32   **GERALDINE: Janie, you've got him staggering! Time for the**

33   **rope-a-dope!**

34   **JANE:** *(Rapid fire, almost never pausing for breath. Throughout her*

35   *lines, JOHN reacts as if pummeled continuously, slowly wilting to*

1 *the floor.)* **I don't see how you can even think of playing golf**
2 **this weekend. You know the gutter needs cleaning and the tile**
3 **in the bathroom has cracked. And besides, you told me you**
4 **had a big project due Monday morning. Plus, you promised to**
5 **take Jimmy to the swimming pool, and Jenny has a recital**
6 **Sunday night, which is the only reason Mom is coming**
7 **anyway. I almost think you care more about Buddy than your**
8 **own family. There's just too much to be done around here for**
9 **you to go gallivanting off to play golf. Why, the house needs**
10 **painting and you still haven't cleaned out the garage, which**
11 **you've been saying you'd do for months now. And I could use**
12 **some help straightening up around here. I don't see why you**
13 **can't do your fair share. Maybe if we had a maid, things could**
14 **be different, but since we can't afford one, you need to take**
15 **your share of the load. Although I can't see why we can't**
16 **afford a maid. Just the other day Mother was telling me that**
17 **she found a lady to clean her house for ...** *(And so on. The*
18 *following lines are said over the "nag session." JANE should*
19 *continue to nag, ad-libbing if necessary, until the exchange*
20 *between BUDDY and GERALDINE is over. When that exchange*
21 *ends, JOHN should interrupt the nag session no matter where*
22 *JANE is in her rant.)*
23 **BUDDY: John! Don't let her nag you!** *(To GERALDINE)* **Hey! What**
24 **kind of rabbit punches are you teaching her to throw?**
25 **GERALDINE: Good clean hits, every one!**
26 **BUDDY: If that's what you call clean, I'd hate to see your laundry!**
27 **GERALDINE: You wanna piece of me?**
28 **BUDDY: Bring it on, sister!** *(GERALDINE crosses the ropes.*
29 *BUDDY is startled; didn't think she'd do it.)* **John! You're**
30 **looking great! Uh ... Catch you Saturday!** *(Runs off, exits.)*
31 **GERALDINE:** *(To JANE)* **Janie, dear, I'll be back to help finish**
32 **him off** *(Points at JOHN)* **as soon as I deal with this weasel.**
33 *(Exits, chasing BUDDY.)* **Come back here, you little coward!**
34 **JANE: ... and another thing, you've been promising for four**
35 **months to ...**

1   **JOHN: I give up!**
2   **JANE: What?**
3   **JOHN: I give up! Your mother can stay.** *(Bell sounds again. Lights*
4   *fade back to normal. ANNOUNCER steps behind curtain.)*
5   **JANE: Really?**
6   **JOHN: Really.**
7   **JANE: For the whole week?**
8   **JOHN: The whole week? Oh, sure, she can stay for the whole week.**
9   *(Beat.)* **In the garage!**
10   **JIMMY: Cool! Rematch!** *(ANNOUNCER steps forward again. JANE*
11   *and JOHN return to fighting stance.)*
12   **ANNOUNCER: Let's get ready to rumble …**

Measure Man

Synopsis: When a thief tries to steal a woman's purse, she is rescued (or so she thinks) by the timely arrival of the Dogmatic Duo: Measure Man and Balance Boy. They quickly tally the thief's sins, present and past, and condemn him to punishment. The woman's delight in this rapid justice is short-lived when the two superheroes begin to list her own failings! As she too is dragged off, we are left wondering how any fallible human can live up to God's standard — absolute perfection. "There is no one righteous, not even one … " (Romans 3:10).

Theme: Who can live up to God's standard of righteousness?

Topics: Christianity, earning salvation, faith vs. works, grace, imperfection, sin

Type: Comedy

Cast: 2 men, 1 woman, 1 older boy/male youth
WOMAN
THIEF
MEASURE MAN — A super hero with an obsession for justice; may wear a cape
BALANCE BOY — Measure Man's sidekick; may wear a cape

Props: Knife, purse, small balance scale, flexible tape measure

Set: Bare stage, or possibly a "Bus Stop" sign on a post.

1   *(The WOMAN is standing Center Stage by the Bus Stop sign. The*

2   *THIEF approaches her, but she doesn't notice him.)*

3   **THIEF:** *(Threatening the WOMAN with a knife)* **OK, lady, gimme the**

4   **purse.**

5   **WOMAN: What?**

6   **THIEF: Are you deaf or just stupid? Gimme the purse!**

7   **WOMAN: But it's …**

8   **THIEF: Shut up!** *(Grabs the purse and knocks her down.)*

9   **WOMAN: Help! I've been robbed!** *(THIEF starts to run when*

10   *MEASURE MAN and BALANCE BOY block his way.)*

11   **MEASURE MAN: Halt, thief!**

12   **BALANCE BOY: Yeah! Halt!**

13   **THIEF and WOMAN:** *(Together)* **Who are you?!**

14   **MEASURE MAN: I'm Measure Man!**

15   **BALANCE BOY: And I'm Balance Boy!**

16   **THIEF: Oh no!**

17   **WOMAN: I'm saved!**

18   **MEASURE MAN:** *(Pulls out a large tape measure.)* **It's measuring**

19   **time! Balance Boy, weigh me this foul fiend's deeds!**

20   **BALANCE BOY:** *(Holds up a scale, puts the purse in it.)* **Stealing!**

21   **MEASURE MAN: Tsk, tsk!**

22   **BALANCE BOY:** *(Takes knife from THIEF, puts it in scale.)* **Armed**

23   **robbery!**

24   **MEASURE MAN: For shame!**

25   **BALANCE BOY: Calling little Suzy Sandblatt a "snot-nosed pig"**

26   **during fifth-grade recess!**

27   **MEASURE MAN:** *(To thief)* **You beast!**

28   **THIEF: What? How did you know about that?**

29   **MEASURE MAN and BALANCE BOY:** *(Together)* **The eyes of**

30   **Justice see everything!**

31   **MEASURE MAN: Vile thief, you have been weighed, measured**

32   **and found wanting!** *(Ties him up with tape measure.)* **Cast him**

33   **to his punishment, Balance Boy!** *(BALANCE BOY grabs the*

34   *THIEF and pushes him through the curtain.)*

35   **THIEF:** *(Wailing in fear)* **Noooo!**

1   WOMAN: Oh, thank you, Measure Man! You've saved me!

2   MEASURE MAN: Not so fast!

3   WOMAN: What?

4   MEASURING MAN: We have not examined your guilt!

5   WOMAN: My guilt? What are you talking about? I'm the victim

6   here! I didn't do anything wrong!

7   MEASURE MAN: I'll be the judge of that! Balance Boy ...

8   MEASURE MAN and BALANCE BOY: *(Together)* It's Measuring

9   Time!

10   MEASURE MAN: Weigh me this flagrant hussy!

11   WOMAN: Flagrant hussy! Why, you pin-headed twerp, where do

12   you get off ...

13   BALANCE BOY: ... Calling Measure Man a pin-headed twerp?!

14   MEASURE MAN: Despicable!

15   WOMAN: What?

16   BALANCE BOY: Peeking into the boys' locker room during tenth-

17   grade P.E.!

18   WOMAN: Hey, wait, that was Suzy's idea!

19   MEASURE MAN: Wanton!

20   BALANCE BOY: Ostracizing Suzy from the popular clique in

21   eleventh grade!

22   WOMAN: Well, you already see how she was misleading me with

23   that locker room incident!

24   MEASURE MAN: Deplorable!

25   BALANCE BOY: Sneaking in after curfew!

26   WOMAN: We all did that!

27   MEASURE MAN: No excuse will save you!

28   BALANCE BOY: Cheating on your econ final!

29   WOMAN: Wait a minute!

30   MEASURE MAN: Do you deny these crimes?

31   WOMAN: I don't deny them, but they're hardly crimes! I'm not

32   like that thief!

33   MEASURE MAN: Wrongdoing is wrongdoing! You have been

34   weighed, measured and found wanting! Away with her,

35   Balance Boy!

1   **WOMAN: No! Stop! You can't do this!** *(BALANCE BOY throws her*
2   *through the curtain.)*
3   **MEASURE MAN: Well, Balance Boy, our job here is done.**
4   **BALANCE BOY: Gee, Measure Man, are you sure about that last**
5   **lady? I mean, she really seemed OK.**
6   **MEASURE MAN: Balance Boy, the standard of justice is**
7   **perfection. Anything less is unacceptable!**
8   **BALANCE BOY: Gosh, Measure Man, can anyone measure up?**
9   **MEASURE MAN: No one can, Balance Boy ... not even you!**
10   *(BALANCE BOY looks suddenly worried.)*

The Miser Touch

Synopsis: An infomercial for the completely paranoid! The "Maxi-Miser System" promises to help you achieve "full-blown, run-for-the-hills, doom-and-gloom financial hysteria." With tips on hoarding, not trusting others and fearing the future, this sketch reminds us that God's power is greater than any fearful doomsday scenario we can dream up.

Theme: Why do we fear the future if God is in control?

Topics: False fears, false prophecies, fear of the future, God's control, God's power, money, talents, trusting God

Type: Comedy

Cast: 1 man, 1 woman, 1 announcer:
CHUCK N. LITTLE — A pitch man (or woman)
HUSBAND
WIFE

Props: Two coffee cups, phone, large purse, sugar bowl, cream pitcher, large paperback book

Set: A plain table and two plain chairs. Two coffee cups, a phone, a large purse, a sugar bowl, a cream pitcher and a large paperback book sit on the table. Slides will appear on the screen throughout as noted.

1   *(CHUCK enters and stands to one side. The WIFE enters and sits*
2   *at the table. The HUSBAND enters.)*
3   **HUSBAND: Hi, hon!** *(Kisses WIFE on cheek, sits at table.)*
4   **WIFE: Hello, dear.**
5   **HUSBAND:** *(Looks in sugar bowl.)* **Honey, did you know we were**
6   **out of sugar?**
7   **WIFE: Out of sugar?**
8   **BOTH:** *(Looking at audience in horror)* **Oh, no!** *(Freeze.)*
9   **CHUCK: Has this ever happened to you? Well, if it hasn't, it could.**
10   **Hello, I'm Chuck N. Little, and I'd like to talk with you about**
11   **Maxi-Miser, the ultimate self-protection system from Fear?**
12   **Yes!** **Incorporated.** *(A slide appears on screen, reading, "The*
13   *Maxi-Miser System. Exclusively from Fear?* Yes!*")*
14   **Let's take a moment to think about all the horrors waiting in**
15   **the daily world:** *(Words appear on screen as he says them, adding*
16   *to a list: STOCK MARKET, HURRICANES, EARTHQUAKES,*
17   *EPIDEMICS.)* **Why, the stock market alone could have you on**
18   **the street tomorrow. But that's not the half of it. Hurricanes**
19   **could cripple the sugar cane industry, leaving you with nothing**
20   **to sweeten your cereal. Earthquakes could destroy Los Angeles,**
21   **eliminating the world's source of aerobic exercise videos. An**
22   **epidemic could strike down workers in the lawn ornament**
23   **industry. Disaster is inevitable.** *(New slide: DISASTER IS*
24   *INEVITABLE!)* **So ask yourself — are you prepared?**
25   *("Maxi-Miser" slide appears again.)* **Well, now you can be,**
26   **thanks to the patented Maxi-Miser formula. With Maxi-**
27   **Miser, you'll learn how to use and abuse the time-tested**
28   **techniques of the world's foremost misers. Here are just a few**
29   **of the secrets we reveal:** *(Each word appears on the screen as*
30   *CHUCK says it. The HUSBAND and WIFE animate and freeze*
31   *with each phrase.)* **Hoarding ...**
32   **WIFE: OK, you distract the waiter and I'll fill my purse with sugar**
33   **packets.**
34   **CHUCK: Mattress stuffing ...**
35   **HUSBAND:** *(Reading)* **A king-size mattress will hold more cash!**

1   *(Slaps forehead.)* **Of course!**

2   **WIFE: Why didn't we think of that?**

3   **CHUCK: Skimping ...**

4   **WIFE: Remember, hon, just three drops of cream. Hoof and**

5   **mouth disease could break out any day.**

6   **CHUCK: Scrimping ...** *(HUSBAND picks up his cup and sips.)*

7   **WIFE: Oh, and I reused yesterday's coffee grounds.**

8   **HUSBAND:** *(Spews. Coughs. Smiles at audience.)* **And still just as**

9   **good!**

10   **CHUCK: Penny-pinching ...**

11   **HUSBAND:** *(Reading book)* **Wow, it even tells how to make Band-**

12   **Aids out of duct tape and cotton balls!**

13   **CHUCK: Don't be fooled; this is not simply sound money**

14   **management or responsible budgeting techniques — we leave**

15   **those for the trusting simpletons of the world. No, Maxi-Miser**

16   **is full-blown, run-for-the-hills, doom-and-gloom financial**

17   **hysteria.** *(New slide: PANIC!)* **Oh, sure, your dollar bills may**

18   **tell you to trust in God, but at Maxi-Miser we say, "Pray if**

19   **you want but keep your eyes wide open!"** *(The COUPLE bows*

20   *heads to pray. WIFE prays with eyes closed. HUSBAND looks up,*

21   *grabs her cup, and drinks quickly. Throughout the remainder of*

22   *the monolog, the COUPLE listens and reacts with pantomime.*

23   *New slide: BUT WAIT! THERE'S MORE!)*

24   **"But Chuck," I hear you say, "I've already got my money**

25   **sealed in watertight Ziploc bags with the gripper zipper and**

26   **the yellow-and-blue-make-green seal, collected in a**

27   **bombproof lead case buried under six feet of premium**

28   _____ *(Insert your state)* **topsoil.** *(The COUPLE nods.)* **Why**

29   **do I need the Maxi-Miser Program?" I'm glad you asked.**

30   **Because the Maxi-Miser Program is not just about money.**

31   **Oh, no. Maxi-Miser covers every aspect of your life. With**

32   **Maxi-Miser you'll learn how to maintain your distance with**

33   **friends and family to avoid the risks of intimacy.** *(The*

34   *COUPLE looks at each other with suspicion and scoots apart.)*

35   **You'll learn to replace your natural ambition with a quivering**

1   **fear of failure. And you'll learn to place no trust in ability or**
2   **knowledge — because with Maxi-Miser, you don't bury your**
3   **talents, you cremate 'em!**
4   **So don't sit around waiting for the future; run from it! Call**
5   **1-800-GUT-LESS today!** *(Slide: 1-800-GUT-LESS. HUSBAND*
6   *picks up the phone and dials. WIFE looks on anxiously.)*
7   **Sorry we cannot accept credit cards, checks, money orders**
8   **or cash. Payment accepted in gold dust, nuggets or non-**
9   **perishable freeze-dried food items.** *(The COUPLE starts*
10   *searching pockets and purse.)* **Sorry, no refunds, exchanges,**
11   **guarantees or warranties. No, we don't trust you either.**
12   **Remember, call 1-800-GUT-LESS today! We might not be**
13   **here tomorrow, and neither might you!** *(The COUPLE looks up*
14   *in horror.)*

Optional Multimedia Presentation for "The Miser Touch"

These cues and slides are intended for use with a multimedia presentation program such as Microsoft PowerPoint. The script cues are listed first, with descriptions of each slide following.

All cues are given by Chuck N. Little (the pitch man). The numbers in parentheses following each cue indicate the slide or effect which should appear. The first number is the number of the slide. The number after the decimal point is the effect. For example, (3.2) would mean slide 3, effect 2.

CUES/SLIDES
Page 92, lines 10–12:
" … I'm Chuck N. Little, and I'd like to talk with you about **Maxi-Miser (1)**,"
　Slide 1: *Text:* Maxi-Miser™
"the ultimate self-protection system from **Fear? *Yes!* (1.1)** Incorporated …"
　Effect 1.1: *Slide in subhead text:* From Fear? *Yes!* ™ Inc.!

Page 92, lines 17–25:
　Slide 2: *Clear Screen. Each text appears flush left, listed from top to bottom as cued.*
　Effect 2.1: STOCK MARKET
" … Why, the **stock market (2.1)** alone could have you on the street tomorrow. But that's not the half of it. **Hurricanes (2.2)**"
　Effect 2.2: HURRICANES
"could cripple the sugar cane industry, leaving you with nothing to sweeten your cereal. **Earthquakes (2.3)**"
　Effect 2.3: EARTHQUAKES
"could destroy Los Angeles, eliminating the world's source of aerobic exercise videos. An **epidemic (2.4)** could strike down workers in the lawn ornament industry."
　Effect 2.4: EPIDEMICS

"Disaster is inevitable (3)."
    Slide 3: *Clear screen. Slide in text from right to left:* DISASTER IS INEVITABLE!

"So ask yourself — **are you prepared? (4)"**
    Slide 4: *Clear screen. Text:* Maxi-Miser™

Page 92, lines 29–30:
" ... Here are just a few of the secrets we reveal:"
    Slide 5: *Clear screen.* Slide in bulleted subhead text, from right to flush left, as mentioned in following effects:

Page 92, line 32:
"Hoarding (5.1) ... "
    Effect 5.1: • Hoarding

Page 92, line 35:
" ... **Mattress stuffing (5.2) ... "**
    Effect 5.2: • Mattress Stuffing

Page 93, line 4:
" ... **Skimping (5.3) ... "**
    Effect 5.3: • Skimping

Page 93, line 7:
" ... **Scrimping (5.4) ... "**
    Effect 5.4: • Scrimping

Page 93, line 11:
" ... **Penny-pinching (5.5) ... "**
    Effect 5.5: • Penny-pinching

Page 93, lines 16–18:
" ... No, Maxi-Miser is full-blown, run-for-the-hills, doom-and-gloom **financial hysteria (6)** ... "
    Slide 6: *Clear screen. Fill screen with flashing red text:* PANIC!

Page 93, line 25:
" ... **But Chuck (7),** I hear you say ... "
   Slide 7: *Clear screen. Text:* But wait, there's more!

Page 94, lines 5–6:
" ... So don't sit around waiting for the future; run from it! **Call 1-800-GUT-LESS (8)** today! ... "
   Slide 8: *Clear screen. Text:* Maxi-Miser™ *Immediately slide in text:* 1-800-GUTLESS

Morning After

Synopsis: Three friends gather in secret to talk about the horrible events of the weekend. Their leader and best friend has been executed, and their comrades have scattered. Even the Governor has spoken out against them. No hope remains until a fourth friend arrives to tell them the grave of their leader is empty.

Theme: What does the Resurrection mean for real people?

Topics: Basic Christianity, Easter (the story of Christ), God's love, grace, hope, Resurrection

Type: Drama

Cast: 3 men, 1 woman:
PETE
TOM
JOHNNY
MARY

Props: None

Set: Modern-day. Bare stage, or could include a cheap table and chairs. A door is optional.

1   (PETE *and* TOM *enter. They look around nervously. They are*
2   *obviously frightened.)*
3   PETE: OK, looks clear, Tom. I don't think the cops know about
4   this place, so we ought to be safe here for a little while.
5   TOM: You think any of the others will show up here?
6   PETE: It's the last place we met before ... Yeah, I think they'll
7   come here.
8   TOM: If the cops haven't grabbed them.
9   PETE: Do you have to be so gloomy all the time?
10   TOM: We may have practically every cop in the city looking for us
11   by now. I've got a right to be gloomy.
12   PETE: Well, keep it to yourself. *(JOHNNY enters.)*
13   JOHNNY: *(Calling out)* Pete? Is that you?
14   PETE: Don't yell out my name like that. It's too risky. And get in
15   here quick before someone sees you.
16   JOHNNY: Sorry.
17   TOM: So where have you been?
18   JOHNNY: I went to the execution.
19   PETE: What?!
20   TOM: Oh, that's great, Johnny. Just lead the cops right to us.
21   PETE: Man, Johnny, what were you thinking? Are you trying to
22   get us all killed?
23   JOHNNY: Well, I couldn't just let him die there alone, could I?
24   What did you want me to do, pretend I never knew him?
25   PETE: *(Angry, defensive)* What's that supposed to mean?
26   JOHNNY: *(Accusatory)* I don't know. What do you think it means?
27   *(PETE and JOHNNY glare at each other.)*
28   TOM: What's going on between you two?
29   PETE: *(Backing down)* Nothing. Nothing at all.
30   JOHNNY: Nothing important now. Anyway, I don't think they're
31   interested in us. They got who they wanted. As far as they're
32   concerned, we're just flunkies. They got the main man —
33   that's even what the governor called him — and the rest of us
34   are just flies on the sidewalk. So relax. Nobody followed me.
35   Nobody even noticed I was there.

99

1 TOM: So ... what was it like?
2 JOHNNY: Horrible. I've seen a lot, but ... the way they treated
3   him, it was like he was an animal — like they were
4   slaughtering a goat or something ...
5 TOM: *(Disgusted)* Yeah. A scapegoat.
6 JOHNNY: And everybody was cheering. I don't know how his
7   mother stood it.
8 PETE: His mother was there?
9 JOHNNY: Yeah. I took her home afterward. I got some of the girls
10   to look after her, then I went to look for you guys.
11 TOM: What about him?
12 JOHNNY: Oh, man. It seemed like it took forever ... it ... I can't
13   imagine what he felt. He cried out once or twice and ... and
14   everyone just laughed, like — like it was all a big show, just
15   for them, you know? And ... and he just hung there, not
16   saying much of anything. I ... I ...
17 PETE: Yeah?
18 JOHNNY: And then it was over. Like that. And everything got real
19   quiet. The crowds, the cops, even the Governor. Like they
20   knew something was wrong but didn't want to admit it. I
21   guess you felt the tremor Friday afternoon.
22 PETE: Almost knocked a wall on me.
23 JOHNNY: Happened right then. It was creepy.
24 TOM: Oh, come on. Coincidence. There was an aftershock this
25   morning. You felt that. You can't tell me it had anything to do
26   with ...
27 JOHNNY: It was to the second, I'm telling you. Scared a cop near
28   me something awful. Scared me too.
29 PETE: What did they ... what did they do with ... you know,
30   afterward ...
31 JOHNNY: They were gonna dump him in a mass grave, but Nick
32   and Joe showed up with a court order. They pulled some
33   strings and got a friendly judge to give them custody of the
34   body. The D.A. was ticked, but there was nothing he could do.
35 TOM: Man, Nick and Joe have some guts. That's not going to win

1 them any friends.

2 JOHNNY: Nick says it doesn't matter. Besides, they're too high up

3 in the social circles. No one's going to risk anything against

4 them — not even the D.A.

5 PETE: So where did you ... bury him?

6 JOHNNY: You know the new cemetery, the one with the garden?

7 Joe has a mausoleum there. Got it for himself and his wife. He

8 offered it on the spot.

9 TOM: Wow. That's an expensive bit of ground.

10 JOHNNY: "Fit for a king," Nick said.

11 PETE: Can I ... is it safe to go see it?

12 JOHNNY: I wouldn't try, Pete. The D.A. ordered a permanent

13 guard on the spot, probably just to spite Nick.

14 TOM: Typical. Like they've got anything to fear.

15 JOHNNY: I don't know. I keep remembering what he said.

16 TOM: Oh, come on, Johnny. He's dead, OK? It's over. The best we

17 can hope is that they don't string us up too.

18 PETE: Lay off, Tom. We know already.

19 JOHNNY: I just keep thinking ...

20 PETE: Yeah. Me too. We all loved him, John.

21 JOHNNY: Yeah. *(There is a long pause, suddenly interrupted by a*

22 *loud knocking. All three start.)*

23 TOM: *(To JOHNNY)* They followed you!

24 PETE: *(Looks as if he expected it.)* Well, this is it then.

25 JOHNNY: No way. I'm telling you, nobody cares about us. Look,

26 it's just Mary. *(MARY enters. She is excited.)*

27 TOM: Did you have to make so much noise? You about gave me a

28 heart attack.

29 MARY: He's not there!

30 PETE: What? Who's not where?

31 MARY: *He's* not! The door was open, and he's gone!

32 JOHNNY: Calm down, Mary. Take it slow.

33 MARY: We went there this morning, to the garden.

34 TOM: Hold on. Who's "we"? And what were you doing?

35 MARY: His aunt Mary and Johnny's mother and me. We went to

101

1   the garden, the cemetery. Everything happened so fast Friday,
2   we didn't have time to do anything but bury him, and the
3   guards and all ... well, you were there, Johnny.
4 JOHNNY: Right.
5 MARY: So we thought, I don't know, we thought we might go there
6   and pay our respects, maybe take some flowers. After what
7   they did to him, we just couldn't let ...
8 JOHNNY: We know, Mary.
9 MARY: So we got there ...
10 TOM: What about the guards? What did you expect them to do, let
11   you in?
12 PETE: Cool it, Tom.
13 MARY: There weren't any guards.
14 PETE: What?
15 MARY: They were long gone. We could see that before we even got
16   there. We didn't know who was going to open the mausoleum,
17   but that didn't matter because the door was already open and
18   the place was completely empty.
19 JOHNNY: Empty?
20 MARY: And then this ... this guy pops up out of nowhere, looking
21   like ... well, looking like nothing I've ever seen. And he starts
22   asking us these weird questions.
23 JOHNNY: What questions?
24 MARY: He says, "Why do you look for the living among the dead?"
25   (Luke 24:5). That's just the way he said it. *(PETE and JOHNNY*
26   *look at each other. PETE bolts Off-stage.)*
27 JOHNNY: Pete! Wait! *(He runs after him.)*
28 MARY: *(To TOM)* Don't you want to see too?
29 TOM: Why? It's just another cruel trick. The D.A.'s probably just
30   trying to flush us out. Look, I realized it was over the moment
31   they put the cuffs on him, and it's high time everybody else
32   came to grips with that. Can't you see? He's gone, OK? He's
33   gone and we're left — we're left with ...
34 MARY: With hope, Thomas. For once, we're left with hope.

The New Guy

Synopsis: The new guy at work meets his fellow employees, only to discover they each have very odd ideas about "The Boss." One claims there is no boss; one says only she knows what the boss wants; one claims there are many bosses, each as good as the next; and the fourth thinks the boss doesn't matter. The new guy reveals he's come to answer all these questions — in fact, he's the boss's son — but the group rejects him.

Theme: What should we believe about God?

Topics: A lost world, attitudes about God, basic Christianity, the Bible, Easter (the story of Christ), faith, false gods, false religion, God's love

Type: Comedy

Cast: 3 men, 2 women:
BETTY — Believes the last thing she's heard: pantheist
BENNIE — Leave-'em-be-Bennie: agnostic
BONNIE — Gloom and doomer: legalist
AL — Cynic: atheist
JAY — The new guy

Props: Coffee pot, cups, doughnuts, thick loose-leaf notebook filled with paper

Set: Stage Right is a door with a sign on it reading "The Boss."

103

1   *(BETTY, BENNIE, BONNIE and AL are standing at Center Stage,*
2   *next to the table. BONNIE clutches a thick notebook and keeps*
3   *glancing at her watch.)*
4   **AL:** I'm telling you, the game was rigged. Do you really believe that
5   penalty was an accident?
6   **BENNIE:** Oh, come on, Al, that's ridiculous. You couldn't get a player
7   to keep quiet about something like that.
8   **AL:** For a million a year I bet I could. That's why I don't go to those
9   games. They're just another scheme to suck money out of my
10   back pocket.
11   **BETTY:** Well, I think you're both right.
12   **BENNIE:** What? Betty, how could both of us possibly be right?
13   **BETTY:** *(Thinks, but not long.)* Well, maybe some of the games are
14   rigged and some of the games aren't and they're all sucking
15   money out of your pocket ... or not ... *(AL and BENNIE look at*
16   *her with utter disgust.)*
17   **BONNIE:** *(Breaks into the group.)* Hey, guys, break time's almost over.
18   We'd better get back to work.
19   **BENNIE:** Lay off, Bonnie.
20   **AL:** Yeah, what's going to happen if we hang a little longer?
21   **BONNIE:** You'd better watch it! You could all be fired!
22   **BETTY:** Why would anybody fire us?
23   **BONNIE:** That's what it says in the manual!
24   **AL:** *(Skeptical, almost sneering)* Oh, it does? Where?
25   **BONNIE:** *(Caught off guard)* Uh ... I know that's in here somewhere.
26   *(She begins to search frantically through the book. The others*
27   *ignore her and settle back to sip coffee. JAY enters Stage Left, looks*
28   *around curiously.)*
29   **BETTY:** Hey, who's the new guy?
30   **AL:** There aren't any new guys in this company, just the same old
31   schmoes with a hair weave.
32   **BETTY:** Well, he looks new to me.
33   **JAY:** *(Comes over to the group.)* Hi, I'm Jay.
34   **BETTY:** I'm Betty.
35   **BENNIE:** I'm Bennie.

1   **BONNIE: I'm Bonnie.**

2   **BETTY, BENNIE, and BONNIE:** *(In unison)* **That's Al.** *(AL waves his*

3   *hand disinterestedly. JAY reaches to shake AL's hand. AL does so,*

4   *but without enthusiasm or interest.)*

5   **BETTY: Welcome to the firm.**

6   **JAY: Thanks. I've been wanting to work here for a long time.**

7   **BETTY, BENNIE, BONNIE, and AL:** *(Surprised, in unison)* **Why?**

8   **JAY:** *(Taken aback)* **Is there anything wrong with the company?**

9   **AL: Is there anything right with it?**

10   **BENNIE: Hey, as long as you don't mind long hours, low pay, a lousy**

11   **medical plan and uncertain retirement prospects, it's a great**

12   **place to be.**

13   **JAY: Surely it's not all bad.**

14   **BETTY:** *(Being positive)* **He's right. I've heard a lot of great things**

15   **about the company.** *(AL and BENNIE glare at her.)* **Of course, I've**

16   **heard a lot of bad things, too.**

17   **BENNIE: So what are you here for anyway?**

18   **JAY: I'm the employee liaison. It's a new position.**

19   **AL: And just what is an "employee liaison" supposed to do?**

20   **JAY: Basically, I take your troubles to the boss, and we take care of**

21   **'em together.**

22   **BETTY, BENNIE, BONNIE, and AL:** *(Totally shocked, in unison)* **The**

23   **boss?**

24   **BONNIE: Oh, we don't want to bother him. There's no telling what**

25   **he might do.**

26   **BENNIE: Hey, as long as he leaves me alone, I'll leave him alone.**

27   **BETTY: Besides, which boss are you talking about? There are so many.**

28   **AL: You're all wrong. There isn't any boss at all.**

29   **JAY: I'm sorry, Al. Did you just say there isn't a boss?**

30   **AL: That's right, "Mr. Employee Liaison." There isn't.** *(To others)*

31   **Has anybody here ever seen the boss?**

32   **BETTY, BENNIE, and BONNIE:** *(In unison)* **No.**

33   **AL: Has anybody ever talked to him?**

34   **BETTY, BENNIE, and BONNIE:** *(In unison)* **No.**

35   **AL: You see? There's no boss. The whole "boss" thing was**

1   dreamed up to keep working stiffs like us in line. Nobody's
2   been able to prove any differently to me, and until they do, I'm
3   not buying it. So you can take your "employee liaison"
4   garbage to some other sucker.
5   BENNIE: Look, I don't care whether there is or isn't a boss — it's got
6   nothing to do with me either way. I'll do my job, and whatever
7   any boss's job might be, he can do his.
8   BONNIE: You guys had better watch what you say. If the boss hears
9   you, you'll be in big trouble.
10   JAY: So at least you think there is a boss.
11   BONNIE: That's right. And you'd better watch your step, because
12   he expects us to obey the rules. I've got 'em all, right here in
13   the company manual.
14   JAY: *(Takes the manual.)* I don't remember the manual being this
15   thick.
16   BONNIE: You need lots of rules if you're going to keep people in line.
17   JAY: *(Opens the manual.)* A lot of these rules seem to be handwritten.
18   BENNIE: *(Leaning over)* And you'll notice that the handwriting looks
19   suspiciously like Bonnie's.
20   BONNIE: There's nothing in there that the boss hasn't said. *(JAY*
21   *looks at her curiously.)* Well, maybe not in so many words. But
22   they're still the rules, and you'd better obey them, or else. *(She*
23   *takes the manual back.)*
24   JAY: Or else what?
25   AL: *(Interrupting quickly)* Don't get her started! *(At the same time,*
26   *BENNIE claps his hand over BONNIE's mouth before she can speak.)*
27   BENNIE: You know, firings, paycuts, layoffs, torture. The usual
28   corporate stuff.
29   JAY: Ahh. Well, what about you, Betty? Do you think we should
30   follow Bonnie's rules?
31   BETTY: Well, Bonnie doesn't have the only manual, you know.
32   JAY: Oh, there are others?
33   BETTY: Oh, sure. Buddy over in accounting has one. And then
34   there's Sam — he's in legal. And, of course, there's Barry. He
35   sort of combined all the rules into one big book. Anyway, I

1   figure you just pick the boss and the rules you like the best,
2   and you'll be fine.
3   JAY: What if the rules contradict each other?
4   BETTY: Oh, you sound just like Al.
5   AL: At least someone around here can think.
6   JAY: Well, it looks like I've started the job none too soon. But if you
7   are willing to work with me, I'm sure we can sort all the
8   confusion out.
9   BETTY: I don't know, Jay. You seem nice and all, but this employee
10   liaison stuff just isn't for me.
11   BENNIE: Look, pal, no offense, but I'll handle my own problems.
12   BONNIE: We don't need an employee liaison if we just follow the
13   rules.
14   AL: *(Skeptical)* Besides, how do you know there is a boss?
15   JAY: Well, he's my dad. *(There is a brief stunned silence.)*
16   AL: *(Sarcastically)* Sure he is. "He's my dad." That's a good one.
17   BONNIE: *(Flipping through the manual)* That's got to be against
18   company rules.
19   BETTY: I'll believe just about anything, but even that's too much
20   for me.
21   JAY: Honestly, he's my dad. In fact, we're having a company party
22   later and you're all invited. If you're interested, I'll come let you
23   know when it's ready.
24   BENNIE: Oh, sure, sure. We're interested. Look, why don't you just
25   go along to Daddy and we'll handle the real work?
26   JAY: Well, it's your choice. Just let us know anytime. *(He walks*
27   *through the door and closes it. The GROUP is silent for a minute,*
28   *then settles back into the doughnut routine.)*
29   BENNIE: If they want to have a party, let them come have it right
30   here, that's what I say.
31   BETTY: I'll bet I can find a better party anyway.
32   BONNIE: *(Looking in manual)* Parties are against the rules. It's right
33   here, see?
34   AL: There's no party. Just work. Pass the doughnuts, will you?

Nothing to Talk About

Synopsis: A young wife is feeling left out by her husband and wants someone to talk with about her feelings. A phone message from a lady at the couple's new church leads her to imagine the results of confiding in someone — but her imagination runs away from her into an ever-increasing spiral of miscommunication and callous gossip. In the end, her fears hold her back from expressing her real needs.

Theme: Who can you confide in?

Topics: Accountability, confidentiality among believers, our need for others, counseling fears, gossip

Type: Comedy

Cast: 5 women, 3 men:
ANDREA — Young wife. Feels like she and her husband haven't been talking much.
BILL — Young husband. Oblivious to Andrea's feelings. Just out for a game of golf.
MARIE — New friend. In Andrea's "fear" sequence, she's just being polite but wants little to do with Andrea.
SUSAN — Marie's friend. A real busybody. Thinks she's a saint-in-waiting.
ALLISON — Andrea's mother. Very proper. Dislikes her son-in-law, despises his mother.
GLORIA — Bill's mother. Can't stand Allison. Has strong religious convictions.
WALTER — Andrea's old boyfriend, and Allison's preferred choice. Wealthy and full of himself. Still has an interest in Andrea. Bill's golfing buddy.
PASTOR FORSYTHE — Bill and Andrea's pastor. Takes his position in society very seriously. A little too quick to judge. Bill's golfing buddy.

Props: An answering machine, several phones, including two cell phones, golf clubs and bag

Set: A chair and end table with a phone and answering machine are Stage Right. Four other small tables or pedestals with phones are spaced across Center Stage, in darkness. Stage Left is bare and in darkness.

**Sound
Effect:** Ringing telephone

1	*(Positioned from Stage Right to Stage Left, next to each phone,*
2	*stand MARIE, SUSAN, ALLISON and GLORIA. WALTER and*
3	*PASTOR FORSYTHE stand in darkness at Stage Left. Lights up on*
4	*BILL near the chair and table, checking a bag of golf clubs. He*
5	*lifts them as ANDREA enters.)*
6	**ANDREA: Where are you going? I thought we'd —**
7	**BILL:** *(Interrupting quickly)* **Can't talk now, hon! Tee time!** *(BILL*
8	*exits, either through curtain or crossing in darkness to stand Stage*
9	*Left between WALTER and PASTOR FORSYTHE. He stands, head*
10	*down, holding his putter.)*
11	**ANDREA:** *(Trails off, disappointed.)* **… spend the morning together.**
12	*(Mildly frustrated)* **Maybe even talk for a change.** *(Sighs to*
13	*herself.)* **It'd be nice to have *someone* to talk to.** *(She looks at*
14	*the phone, sees answering machine message light blinking. She*
15	*presses the play button.)*
16	**MARIE:** *(Off-stage voice)* **Andrea? This is Marie. We've been**
17	**hitting it off so well at church that I thought you might like to**
18	**get together, share a little lunch, talk about life — you know.**
19	**Anyway, give me a shout!**
20	**ANDREA:** *(To herself)* **I certainly have a lot to shout about.** *(Looks*
21	*at phone.)* **What could it hurt?** *(She looks at phone, but does not*
22	*pick it up. Lights dim on ANDREA, and rise on MARIE. MARIE's*
23	*phone rings. ANDREA watches all of the following exchanges*
24	*with concerned interest.)*
25	**MARIE: Hello? Who? Oh, Andrea.** *(Looks at watch, slightly*
26	*annoyed.)* **Sure, I've got time to talk. What's that? Oh, he's**
27	**ignoring you? Going out to play golf a lot?** *(Heard it all before)*
28	**Uh-huh. How long have you been married, honey? That's**
29	**what I thought. Honey, when it comes to golf and men, we're**
30	***all* the other woman. What? Why, of course I'll pray for you.**
31	*(She doesn't mean it.)* **Can I call you back later, Angela? … I**
32	**mean Andrea. Right. 'Bye now.** *(Hangs up.)* **Gee, how needy**
33	**can you get?** *(She looks at phone, picks it up, dials. Lights up on*
34	*SUSAN. SUSAN's phone rings. She picks up.)*
35	**SUSAN: Hello?**

1   MARIE: Susan! I just had to call you. You know that new girl at
2   church?
3   SUSAN: You mean miss oh-right-she's-a-real-blonde?
4   MARIE: That's the one. Well, she just called and started dumping
5   on me about her marital problems.
6   SUSAN: No! She hardly even knows you!
7   MARIE: That's what I'm thinking. Anyway, she starts moaning
8   about her husband going out all the time, feeling like the other
9   woman, and I'm thinking ...
10   SUSAN: Mistress!
11   MARIE: Uh-huh. She thinks it's golf.
12   SUSAN: Well, somebody ought to wise her up.
13   MARIE: I doubt you could wise her up. She was born to be miss
14   last-to-know, if you know what I mean.
15   SUSAN: Well, I work with her mother. Things like this are probably
16   best coming from a parent. Now you're sure about this?
17   MARIE: I have it from the most reliable source.
18   SUSAN: Well, I'll handle it then. I'll let you know what happens.
19   'Bye, Marie! *(Lights out on MARIE as SUSAN hangs up and*
20   *dials another number. Lights up on ALLISON answering ringing*
21   *phone.)*
22   ALLISON: Monroe residence, Allison speaking.
23   SUSAN: Mrs. Monroe, this is Susan Clayton. We work together at —
24   ALLISON: Oh, yes, Susan, I remember you quite well. Please, call
25   me Allison. *(With thinly veiled dislike)* Only my son-in-law calls
26   me Mrs. Monroe.
27   SUSAN: Well, actually I called about your son-in-law.
28   ALLISON: *(With clear distaste)* What about him?
29   SUSAN: Well, I hate to be the bearer of bad tidings, but ... well, I'm
30   concerned for your daughter, and I don't know her that well,
31   and I thought the news might be best coming from you, and I
32   don't mean to be butting in on other people's business, that's
33   just not who I am, but I feel like it's just my Christian duty ...
34   ALLISON: Go on.
35   SUSAN: Well, it seems your son-in-law has been seen going into a

1   hotel with a blonde who is not your daughter. Apparently, it's

2   been happening for a while.

3   ALLISON: The little weasel. I wondered when he'd get around to

4   this.

5   SUSAN: Like I said, Mrs. Monroe, I just feel awful about this, and

6   I'm sorry that I had to be the one to tell you, but I just felt that

7   *someone* ought to know and, well, ... It's just a load off my

8   heart, I can tell you.

9   ALLISON: Thank you, Susan dear. I've been looking forward to

10   this day for six years. 'Bye, now. *(Lights down on SUSAN as*

11   *ALLISON dials. Lights up on GLORIA answering ringing phone.)*

12   GLORIA: Howdy! This is glorious Gloria, and if you've seen me,

13   you know it's true!

14   ALLISON: *(Triumphantly)* Hello, Gloria.

15   GLORIA: *(Less than thrilled)* Oh, hello, Allison. What do you want?

16   ALLISON: I just want to tell you to let your son know he'd better

17   be ready to divvy up the furniture.

18   GLORIA: What are you talking about?

19   ALLISON: I'm talking about his habit of picking up strange

20   women at seedy hotels.

21   GLORIA: I don't believe it.

22   ALLISON: He was seen, woman! They've got photos!

23   GLORIA: A likely story.

24   ALLISON: You know, I think I'll let Walter Jameson know

25   Andrea's free again. He's a wealthy tax attorney these days.

26   Still single too. *(Lights up on WALTER, on a cell phone.)*

27   WALTER: Andrea, baby. I hear you're back on the market. What

28   say we talk about a little merger? *(WALTER now preens and*

29   *talks silently into the cell phone.)*

30   GLORIA: If my little William is seeing someone else, it's only

31   because your shrew of a daughter never learned how to treat

32   a man right. But then, how could she when her mommy's the

33   original ice queen?

34   ALLISON: Why, you two-bit little ... *(Lights out on ALLISON as*

35   *GLORIA slams down the phone. WALTER still preens. GLORIA*

1   *dials. Lights up on PASTOR FORSYTHE, wearing an outlandish*
2   *golf outfit. He answers a cell phone.)*
3   **PASTOR FORSYTHE:** *(Proudly, he likes the title "Doctor.")* **Doctor**
4   **Forsythe.**
5   **GLORIA: Pastor Forsythe! This is Gloria Taylor. I want to know**
6   **what kind of church encourages young men to run around on**
7   **their wives?**
8   **PASTOR: Mrs. Taylor, I assure you we do nothing of the kind!**
9   **GLORIA: I don't know about you, but my son grew up with the**
10   **Ten Commandments. Only now that he goes to your fancy-**
11   **pants church, he seems to think the one about not committing**
12   **adultery ends with "unless you really want to."**
13   **PASTOR: That's a pretty serious charge.**
14   **GLORIA: And I think you need to do something serious about it.**
15   **You're his pastor. Or at least, you're supposed to be.** *(GLORIA*
16   *slams the phone down. If possible, lights out on GLORIA. Both*
17   *WALTER and the PASTOR hang up. Lights brighten to include*
18   *BILL between them. He looks at WALTER and the PASTOR.)*
19   **BILL: If you two are through with your little phone chats, I'd like**
20   **to putt!** *(He notices that both are looking at him, WALTER with*
21   *a superior smile and the PASTOR with an angry frown.)* **What?**
22   *(Lights out on WALTER, BILL and the PASTOR, and up on*
23   *ANDREA. Clearly, she has called no one; it's all in her head. The*
24   *phone rings.)*
25   **ANDREA:** *(Answers.)* **Hello? Oh, hello, Marie. I just got your**
26   **message, and I was thinking of calling you. How's life? Oh,**
27   **you know. Nothing really to talk about.**

The Other Wise Man

Synopsis: Based on "The Story of the Other Wise Man" by Henry Van Dyke. When a fourth wise man stops to help an injured man, he is delayed in his journey to Bethlehem and arrives too late to worship the young Christ. Thus begins a lifelong search for the King of Kings that costs the wise man everything he treasures — but what a reward he finds! Note: This is a slightly longer monolog, running about nine to ten minutes.

Theme: How do we show our love for Christ?

Topics: 1 Corinthians 13, caring for others, Christmas, Easter, faith, following Christ, God's love, living the character of Christ, love, Matthew 26:33-46, serving God

Type: Drama

Cast: 1 man or woman:
STORYTELLER

Props: None

Set: Bare stage

Performance Notes: The storyteller should deliver the dialog in the character of the speakers and freely use gesture, pantomime and expression to present the action of the story visually as well as verbally. Italic type before a quotation indicates which "character" is speaking. Where no italic type appears, the speaker is indicated by the narration.

1   *(STORYTELLER enters and stands at Center Stage.)*
2   **STORYTELLER: In the days when Augustus Caesar was master of**
3   **many kings, there lived in the mountains of Persia a nobleman**
4   **named Artaban. Artaban was a Magi; a philosopher,**
5   **astrologer, healer and priest. His greatest pleasure was to study**
6   **the heavens and seek to know the heart of God.**
7   **One fateful evening as Artaban and his colleagues gazed**
8   **into the night, they saw a new star rising in the West, shining**
9   **brighter than all the stars of heaven.**
10   **"A king is born in Judea!" one Magi cried.**
11   **"Nay, an emperor," cried another.**
12   **"A king who is above all kings!" shouted a third.**
13   **"A Son of God," whispered Artaban.**
14   **That night the Magi made a pact: they would travel to**
15   **Judea to seek the new king, with gifts of gold and jewels and**
16   **frankincense and myrrh.**
17   *(As a Magi:)* **"Let us meet by the ruins of Babylon when the**
18   **star rises again, and we shall journey together."**
19   **And so they parted, each to prepare his gift for the royal**
20   **child. Artaban himself sold all he owned, and purchased three**
21   **gems beyond comparison: a sapphire as blue as a fragment of**
22   **the night sky, a ruby redder than a ray of sunrise and a pearl**
23   **as pure as the peak of a snow-capped mountain at twilight.**
24   *(As Artaban:)* **"Surely the King of all kings will be pleased**
25   **with these."**
26   **And he placed the gems within the folds of his white robes**
27   **and rode to meet his brothers.**
28   **When Artaban arrived on the outskirts of ancient Babylon**
29   **the night was already growing dark, and the star was soon to**
30   **rise. But when he heard a desperate moan of pain echoing in**
31   **the cold night air, Artaban stopped. There beside the road lay**
32   **a Hebrew merchant, his body beaten and raging with fever.**
33   **Immediately, Artaban gave him water and such medicines as**
34   **he carried. But the man required greater care.**
35   *(As Artaban:)* **"If I tarry, I shall miss my brothers. But if I**

1   do not, this son of Judah may die."

2   *(As Artaban, to the star:)* "Forgive me, my King!"

3   And as the new star rose into the sky, Artaban knelt beside
4   the merchant, cooling his brow with water and binding his
5   wounds with strips torn from his own regal robes.

6   It was many days before Artaban could leave the merchant
7   and return to his quest. He was forced to sell the precious
8   sapphire in order to prepare a caravan for the journey.

9   *(As Artaban:)* "One less gift, my King, but I trust in your
10 forgiveness."

11 When at last Artaban arrived in Bethlehem, he searched
12 from house to house, asking about the new King. Some had
13 seen this or heard that, but none knew where the child could
14 be found. At last Artaban found a young mother cuddling her
15 baby boy.

16 *(As Young Mother:)* "Yes, I know who you seek. The child
17 was born in the inn's stable not two days after mine. But the
18 family has gone to Egypt."

19 Artaban thanked the girl and turned to go. But as he
20 reached the door, he heard cries of horror rising through the
21 town, mixed with the sound of marching feet.

22 "They are killing the children!" a woman screamed

23 The young mother swept her child into her arms and looked
24 around her tiny cottage. There was no place for her to hide.

25 *(As Young Mother:)* "Save my son, good father!"

26 "No harm will come to him," the Magi said, and he stepped
27 into the doorway so his body filled the frame.

28 At that moment a troop of soldiers arrived at the house.
29 "Stand aside!" the captain cried. But Artaban did not move.
30 He merely stared silently into his open hand. The captain
31 followed his gaze, and saw a ruby redder than the blood on his
32 sword and brighter than a thousand fires.

33 *(As Artaban:)* "I am resting here alone, waiting to give this
34 stone to the prudent captain who will leave me in peace."

35 *(As the Captain:)* "There is no child here! Move on!"

1   And the officer snatched the gem from the Magi's palm

2   and led his troops away.

3   *(As Young Mother:)* "Oh thank you, kind father! May the

4   Lord our God give you peace everlasting and grant you every

5   blessing!"

6   But Artaban said, "Forgive me, my King. For I have given

7   to evil men that which was meant for God alone."

8   Once again, Artaban resumed his journey, pursuing his

9   King into the ancient lands of Egypt. He went from hovel to

10   hovel, from shepherd's tent to workman's hut, seeking his

11   King. And everywhere he traveled, he also labored, healing

12   the sick, feeding the hungry, comforting the sorrowful. But

13   never did he find the Christ child, nor touch the hand of his

14   prince.

15   The years continued on, now ten, now twenty, now thirty.

16   At last, old and weary, Artaban came to visit Jerusalem. It

17   was Passover, and the streets were filled with Jews from every

18   portion of the world. But strangest to Artaban were the words

19   of the Jews from Galilee, thick with the accent of northern

20   Israel.

21   *(As Man from Galilee:)* "Have you heard? They've arrested

22   him for blasphemy! They say he claims to be the King of the

23   Jews, the Son of God!"

24   *(As Artaban:)* "Please, tell me who you are speaking about!"

25   *(As Man from Galilee:)* "Why, Jesus of Nazareth! He is a

26   rabbi and a prophet of great power."

27   *(As Artaban:)* "Is he truly the Son of God?"

28   *(As Man from Galilee:)* "He heals the sick and gives sight to

29   the blind. Just two days ago I saw him raise a man from the

30   dead! Surely he must be the Messiah!"

31   *(As Artaban:)* "But what is to become of him?"

32   *(As Man from Galilee:)* "They say he is to be crucified by

33   Pilate this very morning."

34   The words struck Artaban like a sword. His King was to

35   die? The One he had sought and served since the star

1   appeared so long ago was to be stretched upon a cross?
2   Artaban reached into his robes, no longer regal as they once
3   had been, and pulled out the single pearl.

4   Perhaps his poverty made the pearl seem richer, or perhaps
5   the years against his heart had polished it to its finest sheen,
6   but the pearl glowed within the Magi's hand brighter than a
7   star of heaven, a gem with price beyond measure.

8   *(As Artaban:)* "At last I may give a true gift to my King. With
9   this I can buy his freedom and save my Lord from death!"

10   But when Artaban arrived at the Roman prison, he saw a
11 piteous sight. A young woman in tattered clothes strained
12 against the grasp of soldiers, who dragged her towards the
13 prison's gaping doors.

14   *(As Young Woman:)* "Have mercy on me, holy Magi! I am a
15 daughter of Persia, far from home. My father has died, and I
16 am sold to pay his debts!"

17   Without hesitating, Artaban held out the pearl.

18   *(As Artaban:)* "Daughter, I buy your freedom! This is the
19 last of the treasures I kept for a king."

20   At that moment thunder rolled across the heavens, and the
21 sky grew dark as night. The ground began to shake with a
22 violent fury, and the soldiers fled in terror. But Artaban had
23 nothing left to fear, no reason to run. He had failed his quest.
24 His treasures were gone, his king was dying. So when a last
25 stone fell from the wall above him, it seemed as if the old head
26 bowed to meet its fate. *(STORYTELLER should bring his fist
27 down upon his head, as if being struck by a falling stone.)*

28   As the girl cradled the dying Magi in her lap, she thought she
29 heard the sound of music, though she could see no one singing.
30 Then Artaban began to whisper, "When, Lord? When did I see
31 you hungry and fed you, or thirsty and gave you drink? When
32 were you sick or in prison and I came to you?"

33   Then the girl heard a voice within the music, saying softly,
34 "Truly I say to you, even as you have done it unto the least of
35 these, my brothers and sisters, you have done it unto me.

1   Come home into your rest, my good and faithful servant."
2   A calm radiance of wonder and joy lit the pale face of
3   Artaban like the first ray of dawn on a snowy mountain peak.
4   His journey was ended. His treasures were accepted. The
5   Other Wise Man had found the King.

Pack Rats No More

Synopsis: A couple is packing up to move to a new house, having promised each other that they won't take anything they don't need. "Pack rats no more!" is their new motto. Unfortunately their motto proves easier to say than it is to follow, as we watch them come up with the silliest justifications for holding on to worthless junk. This sketch takes a lighthearted look at how we carry needless burdens, whether physical or emotional, rather than moving forward in faith.

Theme: Letting go of the past.

Topics: Cluttered lives, fear of the future, holding on to the past, materialism

Type: Comedy

Cast: 1 man, 1 woman:
BARRY — A husband
JANET — A wife

Props: Several large boxes, four "white elephant" objects

Set: Several closed cardboard boxes are Center Stage. The boxes are labeled "Dishes," "Office Books," etc.

1   (*JANET is sitting on the floor in front of the boxes, with a large*
2   *open box beside her. She is taping up another box. BARRY walks*
3   *in carrying another large box.*)
4   **BARRY: OK Janet, here's the last one.**
5   **JANET: Good. Now we're agreed on this, right?**
6   **BARRY: Right. Nothing we don't need goes to the new house.**
7   **JANET: If we don't need it, we toss it.**
8   **BARRY: Toss it all.**
9   **JANET: Pack rats no more!**
10   **BARRY: Pack rats no more!**
11   **JANET: Good. Let's get started. You take that box, I'll take this one.**
12   **BARRY: Deal.** (*He reaches in box, pulls out an item.*) **What about**
13   **this? Looks like a tosser to me.**
14   **JANET: Oh, no, don't throw that out! We could sell that on eBay!**
15   **BARRY: This? Are you kidding?**
16   **JANET: No. People buy stuff like that all the time on eBay.**
17   **BARRY: Really?**
18   **JANET: Yeah. I'll bet someone would pay twenty bucks for that.**
19   **BARRY: OK, if you say so. I'll put it in.**
20   **JANET: Good.**
21   **BARRY: By the way, where did we get that, anyway?**
22   **JANET: I got it on eBay for fifteen bucks. It was a bargain.**
23   **BARRY: Right.** (*He drops it in the box.*)
24   **JANET:** (*Reaches in box, pulls out an item.*) **Now here's something**
25   **we don't need.**
26   **BARRY: Hey! I wondered where that was!** (*He takes it from her.*)
27   **JANET: Don't tell me you want to keep that old thing!**
28   **BARRY: Why not? This "old thing" means a lot to me.**
29   **JANET: If it means so much to you, what was it doing in the**
30   **bottom of a cardboard box in the garage?**
31   **BARRY: Obviously I put it there for safekeeping.**
32   **JANET: Safekeeping. In the garage.**
33   **BARRY: Well, if I left it in the hall closet, you'd have given it to**
34   **Goodwill.**
35   **JANET: Even Goodwill wouldn't take that.**

1   BARRY: They certainly took my letter jacket.
2   JANET: Did you have to bring that up again? I said I was sorry
3   about that!
4   BARRY: I come home, open the hall closet, and my high school
5   letter jacket isn't hanging there.
6   JANET: Please don't go over this again …
7   BARRY: "Honey, what happened to my letter jacket?" I say.
8   JANET: Barry —
9   BARRY: I thought maybe you were having it cleaned. But noooo …
10 JANET: Look, I don't need to be reminded —
11 BARRY: "Oh, I gave it to Goodwill," you say, like it was an old
12   towel.
13 JANET: I said I was sorry!
14 BARRY: My high school letter jacket! The symbol of my glory days
15   on the field of battle!
16 JANET: Barry, you lettered in chess.
17 BARRY: Coach Harris used to say, "It matters not the battlefield,
18   only that the battle's won."
19 JANET: I don't remember you winning that many battles.
20 BARRY: That makes the victories all the more precious.
21 JANET: *(Appeal to heaven)* Give me strength.
22 BARRY: But it doesn't matter now. The symbol of my triumph is
23   gone. The memories fade, lost forever to the —
24 JANET: *(She's had all she can stand.)* Enough! Look, keep that
25   thing, pack it away or display it on the new mantle. I don't
26   care, just shut up about the stupid letter jacket!
27 BARRY: Fine. But it wasn't a stupid jacket.
28 JANET: *(To herself)* It was a moth-eaten old rag, that's what it was.
29 BARRY: *(Pulls another thing out of the box.)* OK, I know neither one
30   of us wants to keep this.
31 JANET: We can't get rid of that!
32 BARRY: What are you talking about? You hate this!
33 JANET: Yes, I do, but your mother gave us that!
34 BARRY: Since when have you been sentimental about my mother?
35 JANET: Look, you know when she comes to the new house she'll

1   look all over for that thing. If she doesn't see it, I'll never hear
2   the end of it.
3   BARRY: You're not thinking of leaving this sitting out!
4   JANET: No, of course not. Just when your mother comes.
5   BARRY: *(Looks over the object.)* Maybe we'll just visit her instead.
6   JANET: It kills me, but pack it anyway.
7   BARRY: OK, it's your decision.
8   JANET: And be careful! We don't want to break it.
9   BARRY: There's a thought!
10   JANET: Barry!
11   BARRY: All right, all right! I'm packing it.
12   JANET: There's got to be something in here we can get rid of …
13   Ah-ha! *(Pulls out another item.)*
14   BARRY: You're not going to toss that out, are you?
15   JANET: Barry, we've got to toss something!
16   BARRY: But we might need that!
17   JANET: For what?
18   BARRY: For an emergency!
19   JANET: What sort of emergency could we possibly need this for?
20   BARRY: I don't know! That's why it would be an emergency!
21   JANET: Barry, we agreed to get rid of anything we didn't need,
22   right?
23   BARRY: Yes. But we might need that.
24   JANET: We can't keep dragging every little thing with us
25   everywhere we go!
26   BARRY: Sure we can. That's why we bought the trailer.
27   JANET: Barry! If we don't toss this, we'll never toss anything!
28   BARRY: You're right, Janet, you're right. We've got to show resolve.
29   JANET: That's the spirit!
30   BARRY: Pack rats no more!
31   JANET: Pack rats no more! *(They high five each other.)* OK, let's
32   load up the rest of this.
33   BARRY: Lead the way, babe. *(JANET picks up a box and exits.*
34   *BARRY picks up the last object, looks at it.)* Still, you never
35   know. *(He puts the object in a box, picks up the box, and exits.)*

The Pedestal

Synopsis: A woman reveals the things that are important to her: money, career and relationships. Each is represented by an object on a pedestal. She proudly displays her idols and compares them to what she sees on everyone else's pedestals: "They're just like mine. Money, Career, Relationships. All our little gods, all in a row." Her story is an honest admission that "where your treasure is, there your heart will be also" (Matthew 6:21).

Theme: What "idols" do we secretly worship today?

Topics: False gods, finding fulfillment, idols, money, values

Type: Drama

Cast: 1 woman:
JILL

Props: A pedestal, a large box, a piggy bank, a desk nameplate, a heart-shaped picture frame with a photo of a handsome guy

Set: A lone pedestal stands at Center Stage. A box nearby contains three items — a piggy bank, a desk nameplate and a heart-shaped picture frame representing Money, Career and Relationships.

1   *(JILL enters and crosses to the pedestal. As she talks, she takes*
2   *each item out and places it on the pedestal, next to the other items.)*
3   JILL: This is my pedestal, my shrine. Like it? It's the place where
4   I put the things I care about — the things that are important
5   to me.

6   Oh, not the things I say I care about. Those are just for
7   show, so I can keep everybody thinking that I'm altruistic and
8   compassionate and "right-thinking." You know, kind of like
9   the answers a beauty contestant gives to those silly "social
10   values" questions: "I believe in the value of world peace and
11   helping inner-city children."

12   No, this shrine is the real deal. This is for the things I
13   actually put my time and energy into. The things I'm willing
14   to make any sacrifice for. Just like you.

15   The first thing I ever put on this pedestal was Money. *(She*
16   *takes out the piggy bank, shakes it loudly and puts it on the*
17   *pedestal.)*

18   You're probably familiar with that one. And why not? Hey,
19   money makes the world go 'round, right? And I found that most
20   of the problems I faced in life could be solved with money. Food,
21   shelter, even friendship. I could have 'em all for the right price.
22   And even when I ran into problems that money didn't seem to
23   solve, I found that tossing enough cash around enough malls
24   could at least keep me from thinking about those problems.

25   At least until the money ran out. Because money runs out.
26   Even plastic has a credit limit, and at some point you have to
27   pay that off. So I had to find another item for my pedestal.
28   *(She takes out the nameplate and puts it on the pedestal.)* Maybe
29   you've heard of it. I called it "Career."

30   The nice thing about Career is, it's more impressive than
31   Money. When I had Money on my pedestal, other people
32   would use words like "greedy" and "snob" to describe me.
33   But when I replaced Money with Career, I suddenly became
34   "ambitious," and "industrious," and even "successful." And
35   the best part is I could still keep Money on the pedestal too; I

1   just kept more quiet about it in public. "Oh, it's not the
2   money," I'd say, and all those admiring people would nod
3   their heads in agreement.
4   Of course, after a while Career got to be lonely. A job won't
5   keep you warm at night no matter how high you can afford to
6   turn up the thermostat. Hey, I'm a red-blooded American
7   woman. I don't want to be alone in the world. *(She takes out the*
8   *frame, holds it up to her cheek and strokes it, then puts it on the*
9   *pedestal.)* So I found another treasure for my pedestal:
10   "Relationships." Because I decided that was the ultimate
11   answer. Whatever problems I faced, whatever unhappiness
12   that Money and Career couldn't cover would be instantly
13   solved if only I could meet the right guy. I mean, that's what
14   we all believe, isn't it? That "Mr. Right" is just waiting out
15   there to make everything perfect for us, and that you've got to
16   be willing to sacrifice anything and everything to find him.
17   And the beauty of it is if one relationship doesn't work out,
18   you can always sacrifice it when the right one comes along.
19   Oh, don't look at me that way. That's what you believe. I've
20   seen you. In fact, I've seen all your pedestals, and they're just
21   like mine. Money, career, relationships. All our little gods,
22   standing in a row.
23   The only difference is, I'm willing to admit it. *(She exits,*
24   *leaving just the pedestal and its contents On-stage. Lights, if*
25   *available, fade slowly to black.)*

Personal Worst

Synopsis: A woman is eager for her first session with a highly recommended personal trainer. Her enthusiasm dims, however, when the trainer begins using insulting chants to "motivate" her to exercise. This sketch looks at the power of words and how positive encouragement is better than negative criticism.

Theme: Our words can motivate or hinder others.

Topics: Encouraging others, the power of positive words, the tongue

Type: Comedy

Cast: 2 women:
JANE — A personal trainer, wears workout clothes
ALICE — Her new client, also wears workout clothes

Props: A clipboard

Set: Bare stage. (Option: workout bench.)

1   *(ALICE is On-stage, stretching. JANE walks in carrying a*
2   *clipboard.)*
3   **ALICE: Hi. Are you Jane Morgan, the personal trainer?**
4   **JANE: That's me, Jane "Good Pain" Morgan!**
5   **ALICE: I'm Alice Fremont. I'm here for my first session.**
6   **JANE:** *(Looks her over.)* **And not a moment too soon, I see.**
7   **ALICE: Gee, thanks.**
8   **JANE:** *(Friendly)* **Just a little joke, Alice. OK, we'll start with some**
9   **general calisthenics, just some jumping jacks to warm up. I'll**
10   **do the cadence. Ready, set, begin!** *(Chants as ALICE begins*
11   *jumping jacks.)* **You're flabby! You're fat!**
12   **There's way too much of that!**
13   **Your bulging thighs**
14   **are twice the size ...**
15   **ALICE:** *(Cuts her off.)* **Hey, wait a minute. What's all that?**
16   **JANE: Motivational chanting. It's one of the techniques I use.**
17   **ALICE: "You're flabby, you're fat"? That's not very motivational.**
18   **JANE: I suppose you came in here because you thought you were**
19   **in perfect shape?**
20   **ALICE: No. I came in to get in better shape.**
21   **JANE: So I'm just adding to your motivation.**
22   **ALICE: If I want that kind of motivation, I'll call my mother.**
23   **Could you try chanting something else, please?**
24   **JANE: No problem. The customer is always right.**
25   **ALICE: Good. I'm ready.**
26   **JANE: Begin.** *(Chants as ALICE starts jumping again.)*
27   **Your hips are like a hippo,**
28   **Your glutes sag like a bag.**
29   **ALICE:** *(Stops jumping.)* **What is that?!**
30   **JANE: It's a new chant. I just made it up. Like it?**
31   **ALICE: No, I don't like it. It's worse than the first one.**
32   **JANE: Well, excuse me. I'm working with limited material here.**
33   **ALICE: What?! I can't believe you. I've half a mind to walk out of**
34   **here.**
35   **JANE:** *(Sing-song)* **Your sign-up fee is not refundable.**

1   ALICE: I know that. Which is also why I'm going to stick it out.
2   That and the fact that you came highly recommended,
3   although I'm beginning to wonder why.
4   JANE: Shall we continue?
5   ALICE: All right. But could you try and be a little more positive
6   with your chants?
7   JANE: I'll try.
8   ALICE: Good.
9   JANE: Ready? Go! *(Chants as ALICE begins jumping.)*
10   I'm positive you're chunky!
11   I'm positive you're huge!
12   ALICE: Hold it! Is that your idea of a positive chant?
13   JANE: Yes. It's got the word "positive" in it, doesn't it?
14   ALICE: That's not the same thing! Look, I came in here because I
15   want to feel better about myself. And your chants are not
16   helping!
17   JANE: Sorry. What would you prefer?
18   ALICE: I'd prefer it if you'd chant something encouraging.
19   JANE: Encouraging?
20   ALICE: Why not tell me what I could be? You know, give me some
21   goals to work for.
22   JANE: Goals? Well, I suppose I could do that.
23   ALICE: Terrific. I'll give it one more try.
24   JANE: Ready? Begin. *(ALICE jumps as JANE chants.)*
25   You could be thin,
26   You could be glam,
27   You could stop looking like a ham.
28   ALICE: That does it! *(She lunges for JANE, who dodges quickly to the*
29   *side. ALICE begins chasing JANE around the stage.)* Hold still!
30   JANE: *(Continuing to run)* You could be slim,
31   You could be trim,
32   You could stop looking like a blimp!
33   ALICE: *(Still chasing)* That's not even a good rhyme!
34   JANE: *(Leading her Off-stage)* That's right! Pick up those knobby
35   knees!

1   **ALICE:** *(Chasing after her)* **I'll pick up your knees, you chanting**
2   **little harpy!**
3   **JANE:** *(Off-stage)* **That's the spirit! Put some passion into it!**
4   **ALICE:** *(Off-stage)* **Auuggh! Come back here!**

Phone Tag

Synopsis: Hoping to find a friend, a lonely man in a "Lost and Found" office calls people listed in an address book. Each call becomes more disastrous than the last, until the worker decides to call the owner who misplaced the book, admitting that "after today, you might want to start a new book."

Theme: How do we find true friends?

Topics: Friendship, loneliness, our need for others, relationships

Type: Comedy/Drama

Cast: 1 man:
MARK GRANT — A lonely guy in a lonely job

Props: Phone, black address book

Set: A desk with a chair behind it. On the desk is a telephone and a sign reading "Lost and Found."

1   *(The sketch opens with MARK sitting behind the desk. He is*
2   *holding an address book and thumbing through it. He stops on a*
3   *page, picks up the phone and dials.)*
4   MARK: **Yes, hello, is Linda there?** *(Brief pause)* **Oh, well, hi Linda,**
5   **this is Mark.** *(Pause)* **Mark Grant.** *(Pause)* **Well, no, you don't**
6   **know me. I just found your name in an address book I picked**
7   **up and called you on the off chance you might know somebody**
8   **named Mark and think I was him and talk to me for a while.**
9   **Pretty pathetic, huh? Hello? Linda? Hello?** *(He looks at the*
10   *phone and hangs up. To himself)* **Well, that didn't work.** *(He*
11   *thumbs through the book some more and stops.)*
12   **Allison ... It might be nice to know someone named**
13   **Allison ...** *(He picks up the phone and dials. Pause)* **Yeah, hi, is**
14   **this Allison?** *(Pause)* **You have a lovely voice, Allison.** *(Pause)*
15   **Oh, my name is Mark Grant. I got your number from ...** *(He*
16   *looks on the front cover of the address book.)* **... Bob.** *(Pause.*
17   *Smiles.)* **Yeah, I guess he is "Mr. Perfect."** *(Nervous laugh,*
18   *pause)* **Well, I don't actually know Bob. I don't actually know**
19   **anybody, really.** *(Pause)* **His address book was turned into the**
20   **lost and found, and there were so many names in it I thought**
21   **he wouldn't mind if I called a few and introduced myself ...**
22   **What was that?** *(Pause, then as if repeating something she's*
23   *said)* **How many names? Oh, gosh, I don't know ... a lot. Bob**
24   **seems like a pretty popular guy.** *(Pauses. Repeats again.)* **Who**
25   **else is in the book? Well, there's Linda ... but you don't want**
26   **to call her, she'll just hang up on you.** *(Pause)* **Yeah, that is**
27   **kind of rude. I don't know what Bob sees in her.** *(Pauses,*
28   *thumbs through book.)* **There's also Michelle and Jennifer and**
29   **Kimberley ... Hey, Kimberley's got five stars by her name!**
30   **You've only got three.** *(Pause)* **What was that?** *(Shocked)* **No, I**
31   **couldn't tell Bob that — I don't even know him! Frankly, I'm**
32   **surprised you'd use that kind of language, Allison.** *(Pause)*
33   **Hey, you were the one who said Bob was "Mr. Perfect."**
34   *(Pause)* **Well, don't blame me for your taste in men. Allison?**
35   **Allison?** *(To himself, as he hangs up and thumbs through book)*

1   Well, I'm not having much luck with the women.
2   **I'll try one of the guys.** *(He dials.)* **David? My name's Mark**
3   **Grant. We sort of have a mutual acquaintance through Bob.**
4   *(Pauses. Laughs.)* **Yes, he is quite the ladies' man ... although I**
5   **think he may be headed for a bit of a slump there.** *(Pause)* **Why**
6   **am I calling? Well, that's a long story. I run a lost and found**
7   **office, and it's kind of a lonely job.** *(Pause)* **Yeah, stuck back in**
8   **a cubicle all day.** *(Pause)* **Yeah, I never see anyone.** *(Pause. He's*
9   *getting depressed.)* **Yeah, no one comes in to talk to me.** *(Quickly*
10   *changing the subject)* **Anyway, somebody turned in Bob's**
11   **address book, and it seemed like he had so many friends and I**
12   **thought he wouldn't mind if I called up and just borrowed a few.**
13   *(Pause)* **No, I've never played golf with Bob. I didn't even know**
14   **he played golf.** *(Pause, brightens up excitedly.)* **Could I join you**
15   **on Thursday? You bet I could!** *(Pause. Tries to be nonchalant, like*
16   *he's not really that desperate.)* **So how good a golfer is Bob?**
17   *(Pause)* **He wins every game?** *(Pause, laughs.)* **Yeah, at twenty**
18   **bucks a hole that could get kind of expensive.** *(Pause)* **You owe**
19   **him how much?** *(Laughs.)* **So that's why Bob wrote "pigeon"**
20   **next to your name. I thought you were just some kind of goofy**
21   **bird-watcher.** *(Laughs, but cuts it off abruptly.)* **No, no. There's**
22   **nothing at all wrong with bird-watching.** *(Pause)* **Hey, it was just**
23   **a joke. There's no need to get all testy.** *(Pause. He's obviously*
24   *getting angry.)* **Yeah, well maybe I am a pathetic, friendless loser,**
25   **but at least I'm not shelling all my cash out because I can't hit a**
26   **stupid white ball with a metal stick.** *(Pause)* **Yeah, well, fine. I**
27   **wouldn't even want to play putt-putt with you!** *(Slams phone*
28   *down. He looks around for a minute, cooling off, then lapsing into*
29   *depression. He buries his head in his hands. There is a long pause,*
30   *then he looks at the front cover of the address book, picks up the*
31   *phone again and dials.)* **Bob? This is the lost and found**
32   **department. I've got your address book.** *(Pause)* **Yeah, the one**
33   **with all your friends in it. Look, about that ... after today, you**
34   **might want to start a new book.** *(Suggesting hopefully)* **My**
35   **name's Mark ...**

Ready for Anything

Synopsis: Todd, an avid technology lover, believes he is "ready for anything" thanks to his array of personal electronic gadgetry. A temporary blackout reveals that his faith in technology is misplaced. The sketch points out the absurdity of viewing technology as an ultimate solution or an ultimate doom; both attitudes reveal a lack of faith in God's promises and power.

Theme: Why do we place our trust in technology rather than God?

Topics: False fears, false gods, false prophecies, fear of the future, God's control, God's power, trusting God, trusting technology

Type: Comedy

Cast: 2 men:
RICK — Todd's friend
TODD — Technophile. Most wired guy this side of a cyborg. Can't imagine life without his technological enhancements.

Props: Tool belt, headphones, PDA (PalmPilot) or some similar-looking device, large cell phone or "Slimline" telephone, various electronic gadgets (the more ridiculous, the better), hat or helmet with "rabbit ear" antennae, several electronic cables, a long orange extension cord

Set: Bare stage, or apartment living room.

1   *(RICK is On-stage, looking at his watch.)*
2   **RICK:** *(Calling to Off-stage)* **Hey Todd, are you about ready? The**
3   **movie starts in about thirty minutes.** *(TODD says something*
4   *unintelligible Off-stage.)* **What was that?**
5   **TODD:** *(Enters. He is loaded down with electrical gizmos of all*
6   *descriptions: cassette recorder, CD player, stereo headphones,*
7   *telephone headset, etc. Around his waist he wears a large tool belt*
8   *from which dangle even more appliances, including a full-size*
9   *Slimline telephone, a power drill, radio, speakers, etc. His hat has*
10   *antennae sticking from it, and he is draped from head to toe with*
11   *cables. An orange extension cord is coiled at his side, with the end*
12   *trailing behind him. As he speaks, he looks at his watch.)* **I said,**
13   **is that Central Daylight Time or Greenwich Meridian Time?**
14   **RICK: How should I know? Thirty minutes is thirty minutes.**
15   **TODD: I'll just punch us in as oh-three-thirty Greenwich. There.**
16   **We're set to go.**
17   **RICK:** *You* **certainly are. What is all that junk?**
18   **TODD: This isn't junk! Rick, you are looking at state-of-the-art**
19   **personal living technology. You can't go through the day**
20   **without it.**
21   **RICK: "Personal living technology"?**
22   **TODD: I am wired for the world, my man.**
23   **RICK: You look like you fell into a Radio Shack clearance bin.**
24   **TODD: Scoff all you want, but with my little arsenal of high-tech**
25   **hardware, I'm ready for any problem the world could**
26   **possibly launch my way.**
27   **RICK: Well, how about this problem? If we don't get in the car**
28   **right now, we won't make it in time to buy our tickets.**
29   **TODD: Hang on a sec.** *(He picks up the Slimline phone, punches a*
30   *number and hangs it up. Then he speaks into the headset.)* **Yeah.**
31   **Two for** *Battle Beyond Infinity.* **That's right, nine-o'clock**
32   **showing. Account number six-oh-nine-three-two. Thanks.** *(To*
33   *TODD)* **There you go. The tickets will be waiting when we**
34   **get there.**
35   **RICK: OK, not bad. But what happens if we run into traffic?**

1   **TODD:** No problemo. *(He pulls out a gizmo.)* **You're looking at the**
2   **new Advanced Global Positioning Satellite Tracker System**
3   **with built-in Enhanced Cartographic Analysis Module.**
4   **RICK: Built-in what?**
5   **TODD: Enhanced Carto — It makes maps.**
6   **RICK: Why would I need a gizmo to make maps? I know the way**
7   **to the theater. We were there last weekend!**
8   **TODD: Ah, but with this baby I can plot out over thirty-six**
9   **alternate routes to avoid traffic jams, road construction, toll**
10   **booths and highway patrol checkpoints. And it tags the**
11   **location of every major fast-food drive-in, should we desire a**
12   **quick bite before the show.**
13   **RICK: Show me.**
14   **TODD: Hang on. I've got to adjust for the proper satellite**
15   **reception.** *(He grabs one leg and lifts it behind him, sticks out an*
16   *arm for balance and tilts his head sideways.)* **There ya go. We**
17   **can shave three minutes by turning left on Hawthorne and**
18   **cutting through the back alley behind Bowl-O-Rama.**
19   **RICK: I'll admit I'm impressed. You certainly seem prepared for**
20   **just about anything.**
21   **TODD:** *(He stands up proudly.)* **You better believe it. At any given**
22   **moment I have direct access to police, fire, search and rescue**
23   **squads and the U.S. Coast Guard. Plus, I've got permanent**
24   **links to twelve different banking services, fifteen major news**
25   **organizations and an on-line self-help guru.**
26   **RICK: Looks like you've got it all covered.**
27   **TODD: You bet. But hadn't we better get going?**
28   **RICK: Lead on, Inspector Gadget.**
29   **TODD: Oh, ha, ha. But when crisis time comes, I'll be ready. There**
30   **is nothing the world can throw my way that I can't handle. I**
31   **am ready for anything.** *(Suddenly the lights go out, leaving*
32   *RICK and TODD only dimly lit, as if by emergency lighting.)*
33   **Aaaah! What happened?**
34   **RICK: Looks like a blackout, Mr. Ready-for-anything.**
35   **TODD: Oh no! What am I going to do? What if the power doesn't**

1   come back on? **I'm lost without this stuff! I've got no satellite,**

2   **no radio, no news link-up. Even the guru's gone dead! I can't**

3   **function! Rick, this is horrible! Our entire technological**

4   **society has just collapsed in one giant ruin! We'll be living in**

5   **caves! Fighting lions and tigers and bears ...**

6   **RICK:** *(Dryly)* **Oh my.**

7   **TODD:** *(Dropping to his knees in terror)* **We're doomed!** *(The lights*

8   *come back on. TODD rises to his feet and acts as if nothing has*

9   *happened.)* **Well, what do you know. Everything's back. News,**

10   **weather, guru. Must have just been a local glitch. You see,**

11   **Rick, with modern technology we have nothing to fear but**

12   **fear itself.** *(He moves to leave, unaware that he has caught his*

13   *extension cord with his foot. He grabs his headphones in panic.)*

14   **Oh no! It's gone again!**

15   **RICK:** *(Picks up cord, hands it to TODD.)* **Relax. You yanked out**

16   **your extension cord. Can we go now?**

17   **TODD: Oh, sure.** *(Nonchalant)* **I'll just plug this in when we get**

18   **there. That way I'll be ...**

19   **RICK: I know. "Ready for anything."** *(They exit.)*

Satisfaction Guaranteed

Synopsis: A radio talk show host promises to help listeners find satisfaction in any situation. However, his advice to one caller, who complains about a bad meal, misses its intended target (a nonexistent restaurant) and hits the caller's wife instead. Her follow-up call reveals that even the host is not "satisfied" with his own life. This humorous sketch shows that "true satisfaction" is not as easy to achieve as the world tells us it is.

Theme: Where do we go for true satisfaction?

Topics: Fulfillment, satisfaction

Type: Comedy

Cast: 2 men, 1 woman:
DR. MIKE — A radio talk show host: smug, intellectually "elite"
HAROLD — A caller
LYDIA — Another caller, HAROLD's wife

Props: Desk microphone or boom mike, headphones, business telephones

Set: A radio broadcasting studio. There is a desk and a chair Center Stage. A large microphone and a business telephone sit on the desk.

Sound Effects: Music — "I Can't Get No Satisfaction"; telephone hanging up, followed by a dial tone

1   *(DR. MIKE sits at the desk, wearing a large pair of headphones*
2   *and speaking into the microphone. HAROLD and LYDIA are Off-*
3   *stage, heard over speakers.)*
4   **DR. MIKE:** *(After "I Can't Get No Satisfaction" plays and fades out.)*
5   **Hello, and welcome back to *Satisfaction Guaranteed*, the**
6   **show that pledges to give you the satisfaction you deserve.**
7   **Have you encountered unacceptable service at a local eatery?**
8   **Is your neighbor's pet wreacking havoc on your prize**
9   **gladiolus? Has your career turned into a brain-numbing**
10   **exercise in disappointment? Then pick up the phone and**
11   **bring your situation to us. I'm your host, Doctor Michael**
12   **Michaels, ready to help you find satisfaction. Let's see who we**
13   **have on the line.** *(Looks at phone, punches a button.)* **Ah, up**
14   **first is Harold from Smyrna. Harold, you're on the air. What**
15   **can I help you with today?**
16   **HAROLD: Well, Doc, the meal I got last night was about the worst**
17   **I've ever had. The meat was underdone, the vegetables were**
18   **overcooked, and the bread was stale.**
19   **DR. MIKE: Ah, a gastronomical catastrophe.**
20   **HAROLD: No, Doc, the food was bad.**
21   **DR. MIKE: Yes, of course it was. And did you complain to the cook?**
22   **HAROLD: You bet I did. I'm not going to stand for that sort of**
23   **service from anyone.**
24   **DR. MIKE: And well you should not. May I ask what was the reply?**
25   **HAROLD: You sure can, Doc. I even wrote it down: "If you think**
26   **you can do it better, you're welcome to try."**
27   **DR. MIKE: The gall!**
28   **HAROLD: Yeah, that's what I thought. And to me, of all people.**
29   **DR. MIKE: Harold, such treatment should not happen to you or**
30   **anyone. It is an affront to gourmets everywhere.**
31   **HAROLD: I guess so, Doc, but I wouldn't know about them. I'm a**
32   **machinist.**
33   **DR. MIKE: Harold, my good man, it matters not what your trade**
34   **is or what status you hold in society, you deserve satisfaction**
35   **and satisfaction you shall get. Listen carefully, and I will tell**

1   you just what to do.

2   HAROLD: OK, Doc, I got my pencil ready.

3   DR. MIKE: Excellent, Harold. First I want you to write a letter to
4   the head of this establishment expressing your great
5   displeasure at the service you received. Do not hesitate to go
6   straight to the top. That's the number-one rule of satisfaction.

7   HAROLD: *(Writing)* Number-one rule … Got it.

8   DR. MIKE: Secondly, print up bills describing both the appalling
9   food and the paucity of service you received, and post these
10   bills in various strategic public locations around town. Be sure
11   to identify the establishment explicitly. If expense is a concern,
12   simple Xerox copies will suffice.

13   HAROLD: *(Writing)* Xeroxes … Check.

14   DR. MIKE: Follow up with a concise letter to the editor covering
15   the same information. Nothing pays off like the effect of bad
16   publicity.

17   HAROLD: *(Writing)* Bad publicity … Good one, Doc.

18   DR. MIKE: Of course. Finally, Harold, a word of friendly advice.
19   Regardless of the outcome, I would advise you never to darken
20   the door of that establishment again.

21   HAROLD: Whatever you say, Doc. But the wife won't like it.

22   DR. MIKE: Well, we can all become attached to places for reasons
23   of sentimentality or past associations of romance or pleasure,
24   but you must explain to her that when the bloom is off the
25   culinary rose, so to speak, it is time to move on.

26   HAROLD: I'll use just those words. She likes pretty stuff like that.

27   DR. MIKE: You flatter me, Harold. Good luck, my good man. I
28   hope you find another restaurant that serves you better.

29   HAROLD: Restaurant? I'm talking about my wife's cooking.
30   Thanks, Doc. I'm going to start following your suggestions
31   right now.

32   DR. MIKE: *(Realizing he's made a horrible mistake, trying to*
33   *interrupt)* Harold —

34   HAROLD: *(Interrupting DR. MIKE)* Oh, it don't make no
35   difference. Bad service is bad service, right Doc? 'Bye now!

1   **DR. MIKE: Wait, Harold! Don't …** *(The sound of a phone hanging*
2   *up, followed by a dial tone, is heard.)* **We seem to have lost**
3   **Harold. Harold, if you're still listening, I recommend that you**
4   **refrain from following my advice with regards to your wife.**
5   **Otherwise, I guarantee you will not receive much satisfaction,**
6   **although I daresay you will definitely get what you deserve.**
7   **Well, let's move on, shall we? On the line we have …** *(Looks*
8   *at phone.)* **Well it looks like we have another call from Smyrna.**
9   *(Punches a button.)* **Hello, Lydia from Smyrna, how can we**
10   **satisfy you today?**
11   **LYDIA: You can start by shutting your big yap.**
12   **DR. MIKE: I beg your pardon?**
13   **LYDIA: Where do you get off telling my husband all that garbage**
14   **about letters to the editor and not darkening my door again?**
15   **DR. MIKE: Ah, you must mean Harold.**
16   **LYDIA: Of course I mean Harold. I barely get into the first three**
17   **minutes of *Oprah* when Harold comes strolling in from the**
18   **garage blabbing about "sending mental kitties" and "killing**
19   **off the roses."**
20   **DR. MIKE: I believe that's "sentimentality" and "culinary rose."**
21   **LYDIA: I don't care if it's daffodils in April, the man's jabbering**
22   **on like a guest on *Sally Jesse Raphael*, and it's all your fault.**
23   **DR. MIKE: Lydia, my good woman, please try to calm yourself.**
24   **LYDIA: Calm myself? Right now my husband's out plastering**
25   **every utility pole in sight with my picture and a sign that says**
26   **"Wanted for murdering the meatloaf," and you're telling me**
27   **to calm myself?**
28   **DR. MIKE: My sincere apologies, madam, but your husband did**
29   **give me the distinct impression that you were a restaurateur.**
30   **LYDIA: Don't you start that name-calling with me, you stuffed bag**
31   **of wind. "Satisfaction Guaranteed" my sweet Aunt Fanny.**
32   **Why, if all your suggestions were made of water, they still**
33   **wouldn't satisfy a cactus.**
34   **DR. MIKE:** *(Losing both his composure and his "intellectual"*
35   *persona)* **Now listen here, lady, you think I enjoy having to sit**

1 here every day and listen to all the whiny little complaints
2 from dolts like your husband? *(Whines.)* "My food tastes bad,"
3 "My water's cold," "My boss stinks." Blah, blah-blah, blah-
4 blah. You think I find this stuff even remotely satisfying? I
5 could be off on the lecture circuit, raking in the dough from
6 rich blue-haired hypochondriacs, but noooo, thanks to that
7 imbecilic agent of mine I'm locked into a contract that keeps
8 me tied to this microphone day in and day out, my only source
9 of conversation coming from intellectual giants like your
10 husband Harold who, I might add, would not even have called
11 here were you not such a horrible cook! So good-bye, Lydia,
12 and in the future stick to serving cereal! *(He punches the phone*
13 *button angrily. He pauses briefly, realizing what he's just done,*
14 *and collects himself.)* Well, listeners, I don't know about you,
15 but I found that immensely satisfying. This is Doctor Mike,
16 signing off and saying, if you're not satisfied, don't blame me.
17 *(Music fade up: "I Can't Get No Satisfaction." Fade out.)*

The Second Coming Kit

Synopsis: An infomercial urges the audience to purchase the Second Coming Kit so they can be adequately prepared for the "Day of Wrath." The kit includes a "Rapture Hook," a "Holy Watchman Alarm Clock," a "Mark of the Beast Eraser" and more. This sketch exposes the ridiculous fears Christians often have about what should be seen as a joyous promise rather than a terrifying threat.

Theme: How should Christians prepare for "The Last Day"?

Topics: False fears, fear of the future, God's faithfulness, grace, Judgment Day, Revelation, salvation

Type: Comedy

Cast: 2 men, 1 woman:
WIFE
HUSBAND
ANNOUNCER

Props: A notebook computer, a newspaper, two champagne glasses (filled), a large box labeled "Second Coming Kit," an umbrella handle or cane attached to a utility belt, an alarm clock, a large eraser, a pocket mirror, ear muffs, a large folded map, a "Viewmaster" toy slide viewer, a book, a bookmark

Set: A living room: Sofa or two chairs, coffee table. There is a notebook computer on the coffee table (closed at first). A large box sits to the side of the sofa. The box has "Second Coming Kit" printed on it, but the printed side is not visible to the audience. A newspaper hangs on one arm of the sofa.

Sound Effects: Ringing alarm clock

1   *(The WIFE sits on the sofa, watching an imaginary TV. The*
2   *HUSBAND enters carrying champagne glasses. The ANNOUNCER*
3   *stands to the side, in the dark, facing away from the audience.)*
4   **WIFE: Honey! Come quick! Dick Clark is on!**
5   **HUSBAND: I've got the bubbly!**
6   **WIFE: Champagne?**
7   **HUSBAND: Relax, it's sparkling cider.**
8   **WIFE: Oh, look, the countdown's started!**
9   **BOTH: Ten, nine, eight, seven, six, five, four, three, two ...** *(They*
10 *freeze.)*
11 **ANNOUNCER:** *(Turns to face audience, steps into light.)* **Yes, the**
12 **time has finally arrived. The clock is ticking. The ball is**
13 **dropping. The end of the year draws near. And as you sit at**
14 **home naively celebrating with your loved ones, we at Pious**
15 **Panic, Inc. have only one question to ask: Are you ready for**
16 **Judgment Day?** *(Multimedia slide: ARE YOU READY? The*
17 *HUSBAND and WIFE start moving, reacting in fear to what he*
18 *says.)* **Yes, it's come upon you sooner than you expected, faster**
19 **than you'd dreamed: The Last Days! The End of Time! The**
20 **Doom of the Earth!**
21   **We're talking nothing short of the Complete and Final**
22 **Apocalypse!** *(Multimedia, flashing: APOCALYPSE!)*
23 **HUSBAND: Auuughh!**
24 **ANNOUNCER: Screaming won't do any good.** *(Multimedia:*
25 *SCREAMING, "Xed" out. WIFE begins crying.)* **Crying's out**
26 **too.** *(Multimedia: CRYING, "Xed" out. HUSBAND and WIFE*
27 *begin praying.)* **And it will be much too late for that.**
28 *(Multimedia: PRAYING, "X-ed" out.)*
29 **HUSBAND and WIFE:** *(Together)* **What do we do?!**
30 **ANNOUNCER: But there's still hope. The Day of Doom is not**
31 **here ... yet. There's still time to prepare with the Second**
32 **Coming Kit, the official survival supplement of the Day of**
33 **Wrath!** *(Multimedia, flashing: SECOND COMING KIT! Slide in*
34 *subtext: FROM PIOUS PANIC, INC. The HUSBAND pulls a large*
35 *box labeled "Second Coming Kit" from beside the couch. He*

1   *starts pulling things out of the box — the alarm clock, the eraser*

2   *and mirror, but not the Rapture Hook.)* **Let's take a moment to**

3   **examine all the advantages the Second Coming Kit has to**

4   **offer. Revelation tells us that believers will be swept into**

5   **heaven when our Lord returns. But what if in the chaos of**

6   **that joyous moment the Heavenly Eye should overlook your**

7   **hapless soul? Are you certain you won't be left behind? Well,**

8   **have no fear, because you'll always be ready for that heavenly**

9   **hook-up with the Second Coming Rapture Hook.** *(Multimedia:*

10   *RAPTURE HOOK.)*

11   *(HUSBAND pulls Rapture Hook — an umbrella handle or*

12   *cane with a belt — out of the box, admires it, and buckles it on*

13   *around his chest so the hook is above his head.)* **Made of sturdy**

14   **oak, each Rapture Hook is lovingly carved by master**

15   **craftsmen, then anointed with natural oils by representatives**

16   **from every major Christian denomination. Rest assured,**

17   **when the Rapture comes, the Divine Hand can't help but get**

18   **a solid grip on this.**

19   **WIFE:** *(Looking in box)* **Don't I get one?**

20   **HUSBAND: Sorry, hon. There's just the one.**

21   **WIFE: I don't want to be left behind!**

22   **HUSBAND: I know! We'll hold hands!** *(They do. WIFE looks unsure.)*

23   **ANNOUNCER: But that's not all. Scriptures tell us to always be**

24   **watchful. God forbid your eyelids should droop when the**

25   **heavenly call sounds.** *(HUSBAND falls asleep with head on the*

26   *newspaper. WIFE is reading.)* **Well, the Holy Watchman Alarm**

27   **Clock will wake you every fifteen minutes so you won't be**

28   **caught napping at the moment of Judgment.** *(Multimedia:*

29   *HOLY WATCHMAN ALARM CLOCK. Alarm clock rings. WIFE*

30   *bends over to pick something up.)*

31   **HUSBAND:** *(Wakes up, doesn't see her.)* **Whaaa? Sarah? She's**

32   **gone! I've missed the Rapture!**

33   **WIFE:** *(Standing up.)* **Relax, I just dropped my bookmark.**

34   **ANNOUNCER: And we mustn't forget the darker side of the final**

35   **days. You can be on guard against the ultimate evil with our**

1	exclusive Antichrist Identity Indicator on CD-ROM. *(Multimedia:*
2	*ANTICHRIST INDICATOR CD-ROM. HUSBAND opens*
3	*notebook computer, begins typing.)* **Using the latest millennial**
4	**technology, we've compiled a complete database of the world's**
5	**political and cultural leaders.** *(Multimedia slide in sub-bullet*
6	*point: With Beast-O-Meter!)* **Just feed the data into our**
7	**patented Beast-O-Meter, and you'll get instant analysis**
8	**charting the likelihood that your favorite celebrity is actually**
9	**the Spawn of Darkness.**
10	**HUSBAND:** *(Points to screen.)* **Whoa! Look, honey, _____**
11	*(Insert a current male celebrity)* **just shot up twelve points!**
12	**WIFE:** *(Looking over his shoulder)* **I never knew he had horns.**
13	**ANNOUNCER: Plus, protect yourself even further with the Mark**
14	**of the Beast Eraser and handy pocket mirror.** *(Multimedia:*
15	*MARK OF THE BEAST ERASER.)*
16	**HUSBAND:** *(Looks in mirror.)* **Aaaah! Quick, I've got the mark!**
17	**I've got the mark!**
18	**WIFE:** *(Examines his forehead.)* **Relax, dear. Remember, you fell**
19	**asleep on the newspaper. It's just some ink from this picture**
20	**of _____.** *(Insert current political or entertainment figure.)*
21	**HUSBAND: Aaaah! Erase it! Erase it!** *(They rub furiously.)*
22	**ANNOUNCER: It doesn't end here. You'll also get the Concise**
23	**Map of the New Jerusalem, the Gabriel's Trumpet Ear**
24	**Protectors and the entire** *Left Behind* **series on microfiche!**
25	*(Multimedia: MAP, EAR PROTECTORS, LEFT BEHIND*
26	*SERIES. HUSBAND lifts out a large folded map, a pair of thick*
27	*earmuffs and a Viewmaster toy viewer. He presses viewer to his*
28	*eyes, looks up at lights.)*
29	**WIFE: Time for dinner, honey.**
30	**HUSBAND: Sorry, I can't put this down.**
31	**WIFE: It's that good?**
32	**HUSBAND: Well, the book's OK, but I've been squinting so long**
33	**my eyelids are stuck to the viewer.** *(She tries to help him pull the*
34	*viewer away from his face as the ANNOUNCER continues.)*
35	**ANNOUNCER: Yes, the Second Coming Kit has everything you**

1   **need for your entrance to Eternity. Order yours today ...**
2   **before you're left behind!** *(Multimedia: SECOND COMING*
3   *KIT. ORDER NOW!)*

Optional Multimedia Presentation for "The Second Coming Kit"

These cues and slides are intended for use with a multimedia presentation program such as Microsoft PowerPoint. The script cues are listed first, with descriptions of each slide following.

All cues are given by the Announcer. The numbers in parentheses following each cue indicate the slide or effect that should appear. The first number is the number of the slide. The number after the decimal point is the effect. For example, (3.2) would mean slide 3, effect 2.

CUES/SLIDES

The words in bold type are your cues from the script. Click to the next slide (or effect) when these words are spoken.

Page 144, lines 15–16:
" ... Are you ready for **Judgment Day? (1)** ... "
   Slide 1: *Text:* Are you ready?

Page 144, lines 21–22:
" ... We're talking nothing short of the **Complete and Final Apocalypse! (2)"**
   Slide 2: *Clear screen. Flashing text:* APOCALYPSE!

Page 144, line 24:
"Screaming won't do any **good. (3, 3.1)"**
   Slide 3: *Clear screen. Text:* SCREAMING
   Effect 3.1: *A large "X" appears on the word "SCREAMING"*

Page 144, lines 25–26:
"Crying's out **too. (4, 4.1)"**
   Slide 4: *Clear screen. Text:* CRYING
   Effect 4.1: *A large "X" appears on the word "CRYING"*

Page 144, line 27:
"And it will be much too late for **that. (5, 5.1)**"
   Slide 5: *Clear screen. Text:* PRAYING
   Effect 5.1: *A large "X" appears on the word "PRAYING"*

Page 144, lines 31–32:
"..There's still time to prepare, with the **Second Coming Kit, (6, 6.1)** ... "
   Slide 6: *Clear screen. Flashing text:* SECOND COMING KIT!™
   Effect 6.1: *Slide in subtext:* FROM PIOUS PANIC, INC.

Page 145, lines 8–9:
" ... ready for that heavenly hook up with the Second Coming **Rapture Hook (7)** ... "
   Slide 7: *Clear screen. Text:* RAPTURE HOOK

Page 145, lines 26–27:
" ... Well, the **Holy Watchman Alarm Clock (8) will** ... "
   Slide 8: *Clear screen. Text:* HOLY WATCHMAN ALARM CLOCK

Page 146, line 1:
" ... ultimate evil with our exclusive **Antichrist Identity Indicator (9)** on CD-ROM ... "
   Slide 9: *Clear screen. Text:* ANTICHRIST INDICATOR
   Slide in subhead text, from right to flush left:

Page 146, lines 6–7:
" ... Just feed the data into our patented **Beast-O-Meter (9.1)** ... "
   Effect 9.1: With Beast-O-Meter!

Page 146, lines 13–14:
" ... protect yourself even further with the **Mark of the Beast Eraser (10)**"
   Slide 10: *Clear screen. Text:* MARK OF THE BEAST ERASER
   Slide in subhead text, from right to flush left:
"and handy **pocket mirror (10.1)** ... "
   Effect 10.1: Includes free mirror!

Page 146, lines 22–24:
   Slide 11: *Clear screen. Slide in bulleted text, from right to flush left:*

" … It doesn't end here. You'll also get the **Concise Map (11.1)** of the New Jerusalem,"

> **Effect 11.1:** MAP OF THE NEW JERUSALEM!

"the Gabriel's Trumpet **Ear Protectors, (11.2)**"

> **Effect 11.2:** EAR PROTECTORS!

"and the entire *Left Behind* **(11.3)** series … "

> **Effect 11.3:** *LEFT BEHIND* SERIES!

Page 146, line 35–page 147, line 1:

"Yes, the **Second Coming Kit (12)**"

> **Slide 12:** *Clear screen. Text:* SECOND COMING KIT!™

"has everything you need for your entrance to **eternity (12.1) …** "

> **Effect 12.1:** *Flashing subtext:* ORDER NOW!

Stop Me, or I'll Quit Again!

Synopsis: A man attends his first meeting of "Quitters Anonymous" and tells the story of his life as a quitter, encouraged by his fellow "Q.A." members. The sketch looks at how we turn little fears into big obstacles.

Theme: How do we handle obstacles in life?

Topics: Commitment, fear of failure, fulfillment, making the most of life, quitting, self-discipline, success, talents

Type: Comedy

Cast: 1 man, 4 (or more) mixed:
BOB — A quitter
QUITTERS 1–3 *(more optional)*

Props: None

Set: A podium, a microphone and several folding chairs. A large sign reads "Quitters Anonymous."

1   *(The QUITTERS enter, setting up more folding chairs, greeting*
2   *each other, etc. After they are seated, BOB enters nervously.*
3   *QUITTER 1 waves him over to a seat, then stands to go to the*
4   *podium and address the group.)*
5   **QUITTER 1:** **I'm glad everybody could make it to Q.A. tonight. I**
6   **heard some talk about quitting early; I think that's a**
7   **temptation we should avoid, don't you?** *(The other QUITTERS*
8   *look a little ashamed.)* **Now, let's begin with some sharing. We**
9   **have someone new to start us off tonight, and I'll let him**
10   **introduce himself.** *(Waves BOB over to the podium, then returns*
11   *to her seat.)*
12   **BOB:** *(Steps up to the podium and taps the microphone. He's nervous*
13   *and unsure.)* **Uh, hello. My, uh, my name is Bob.**
14   **QUITTERS 1, 2, 3, etc.:** *(In unison)* **Hi, Bob!**
15   **BOB:** *(Emboldens himself.)* **My name is Bob ...**
16   **QUITTERS 1, 2, 3, etc.:** *(In unison)* **Hi, Bob!**
17   **BOB:** **Hi. Like I was saying, my name ...** *(Realizes they're going to*
18   *"Hi Bob" him again, and stops himself.)* **Uh, hi. I'm a quitter.**
19   **QUITTER 1:** **You've come to the right place.**
20   **QUITTER 2:** **You're among friends, Bob.**
21   **QUITTER 3:** **Tell us more about it, Bob.**
22   **BOB:** **I guess it all started when I was a kid. I was playing on a**
23   **Little League team, but the practices were so hard and I**
24   **couldn't hit the ball and, well, when the coach didn't put me**
25   **in the starting line-up, I just walked away. Oh, I'd heard the**
26   **warnings: "Quitters never win," "You don't get ahead by**
27   **staying behind." But it felt so good, you know? And once I**
28   **started quitting, I started finding reasons to do it again. Any**
29   **time something got difficult, any time I felt things were unfair,**
30   **I'd just give up. It was so much easier. And I liked it.**
31   **Pretty soon I was quitting everything. I quit the Cub**
32   **Scouts, the children's choir, piano lessons. I even started**
33   **joining clubs just so I could quit ... I'm so ashamed.**
34   **QUITTER 2:** **It's OK, Bob. You can tell us anything.**
35   **BOB:** **I even quit the Mickey Mouse Club!** *(The QUITTERS all nod*

1   *in sympathy.)*

2   **QUITTER 1: We've been there, Bob.**

3   **BOB: It got worse as I got older. I was in denial; I started using all**

4   **the old excuses, saying anything to explain away my habit.**

5   **"Quit while you're ahead," "Quit while the quitting's good,"**

6   **"It's quitting time!" When someone told me to quit making**

7   **excuses, I did!** *(Breaks down, then regathers composure.)*

8   **I was pretty far gone at that point. I started to look for my**

9   **quitting fix everywhere. I quit the Columbia House Record**

10   **Club so many times, they started mailing back my pennies. I**

11   **guess that's when I first realized I had a problem. Oh, I tried**

12   **to deny it. I'd tell myself I wasn't quitting, I was just making**

13   **an "alternative participation choice." Finally, when I decided**

14   **to quit worrying about it, I realized how low I'd gotten. I**

15   **couldn't quit quitting! It was an endless cycle!**

16   **So I tried to come up with a way to break the cycle on my**

17   **own. I decided that if I wasn't doing something, I couldn't**

18   **quit it. That's when I began not starting things.**

19   **QUITTER 3: Same song, second verse.**

20   **BOB: Whenever I saw an opportunity, I'd just let it pass. After all,**

21   **I said to myself, what if the opportunity didn't work out?**

22   **What if I couldn't meet the goals? Then I'd just have to quit**

23   **again. I told myself the temptations were just too great. So**

24   **rather than wait for difficulty to enter my life, I just avoided**

25   **it all together. It seemed like the perfect solution.**

26   **QUITTER 2: It always does.**

27   **BOB: But that was a lie. It turned out that not starting things was**

28   **just another form of quitting. It didn't help, it just made my**

29   **problems worse. I stayed in a dead end job because I quit**

30   **pursuing better things. I stayed out of relationships because I**

31   **was afraid I'd have to quit them later. I stopped calling my**

32   **mother because at the end of the conversation I'd have to quit**

33   **talking. I hadn't quit quitting, I'd just quit living.**

34   **QUITTER 1: Amen.**

35   **BOB: So here I am at Quitter's Anonymous — Me, Bob!**

1   QUITTERS 1, 2, 3, etc.: *(In unison)* **Hi, Bob!**
2   **BOB: I'm here to get my life in order, to start doing things and**
3   **never stop.**
4   QUITTERS 1, 2, 3, etc.: *(In unison)* **Yesiree, Bob!**
5   **BOB: With your help I know I'll be able to say, "As God is my**
6   **witness, I'll never quit again"** *(The QUITTERS stand and*
7   *applaud.)* **Besides, if this doesn't work out, I can always quit.**
8   *(The QUITTERS look dismayed.)*

The Subject

Synopsis: A researcher encounters a subject with a tendency for strong emotional reactions to the most trivial events. The subject's behavior becomes increasingly absurd until the researcher quits in complete frustration — only who is actually studying whom? A comedy with a surprising twist, this sketch demonstrates how our emotions can override our judgment in illogical ways.

Theme: Letting emotions get the best of us.

Topics: Emotions, self-control, self-discipline

Type: Comedy

Cast: 1 man, 1 man or woman:
RESEARCHER — Can be male or female
MR. MERRIL — Subject

Props: Box of yellow pencils, clipboard, lab coat

Set: A desk with two chairs, one on either side of the desk. The box of yellow pencils should be inside the desk for use in the sketch.

1   *(MR. MERRIL is sitting in one of the chairs, waiting expectantly.*

2   *The RESEARCHER enters, wearing a white lab coat and carrying*

3   *a clipboard.)*

4   **RESEARCHER:** *(Looking at clipboard)* **Mr. ... Merril, is it?**

5   *(Pronounces the name "MER-ril.")*

6   **MR. MERRIL:** *(Very friendly)* **It's Mer-*ril*. You put the accent on**

7   **the *ril*.**

8   **RESEARCHER:** *(Sits in the other chair.)* **Well, Mr. Mer-*ril*, thank**

9   **you for agreeing to be part of our study.**

10   **MR. MERRIL: No problem. So, whatcha studying?**

11   **RESEARCHER: I'm sorry, I can't tell you that. It could skew the**

12   **results of the study.**

13   **MR. MERRIL: I gotcha. Gotta be scientific and all that.**

14   **RESEARCHER: And all that, yes. We're going to start with a little**

15   **word association game. I'll say a word and you just say the**

16   **first thing that comes to your mind.**

17   **MR. MERRIL: Okey-dokey.**

18   **RESEARCHER:** *(Looking in desk)* **Now, let me get a pencil ...**

19   **MR. MERRIL:** *(Suddenly howls with anguish)* **Noooo! My pencil,**

20   **my poor pencil!** *(He buries his head on the desk, sobbing.)*

21   **RESEARCHER:** *(Stunned)* **Mr. Mer-*ril*, what's wrong?**

22   **MR. MERRIL: I just thought of my favorite pencil, the one I had**

23   **as a boy. But it's lost now, gone, gone ...**

24   **RESEARCHER: Now, calm down, Mr. Mer-*ril*. Maybe you should**

25   **tell me about it.**

26   **MR. MERRIL:** *(Still sad)* **Oh, it was beautiful. It was made of wood**

27   **and painted a bright golden yellow. On one end it had a**

28   **wonderful piece of red rubber you could use to erase mistakes.**

29   **And there were words engraved on it, the most beautiful**

30   **words I've ever read.**

31   **RESEARCHER:** *(During the previous speech finds and examines a*

32   *pencil. Reads.)* **"Ticonderoga Number Two"?**

33   **MR. MERRIL:** *(Looks up, surprised.)* **Yes! How could you know that?**

34   *(Sees the pencil.)* **My pencil!** *(Suddenly enraged)* **You took it!**

35   *(Grabs pencil.)* **Give me that! You thief! You — you hoodlum!**

1   RESEARCHER: Mr. Mer-*ril*, calm down. I assure you, that is not
2   your pencil.
3   MR. MERRIL: Yes it is! How could you say that?! You're a thief
4   and a liar!
5   RESEARCHER: *(Reaches in desk, pulls out a box of pencils.)* No,
6   look, I have a whole box of pencils just like that one.
7   MR. MERRIL: *(Calms completely — he's amazed.)* A whole box?
8   RESEARCHER: Yes, Mr. Merril. *(Pronounces it MER-ril.)*
9   MR. MERRIL: *(Friendly again)* Mer-*ril*.
10   RESEARCHER: Whatever — A whole box of yellow Ticonderoga
11   Number Two pencils.
12   MR. MERRIL: With red erasers?
13   RESEARCHER: With red erasers.
14   MR. MERRIL: Can I have one?
15   RESEARCHER: *(Willing to try anything)* You can have the whole
16   box.
17   MR. MERRIL: *(Overjoyed, clutches the box and a handful of
18   pencils.)* Oh, how wonderful. I take back everything I said
19   about you. You are truly a wonderful human being.
20   RESEARCHER: *(Relieved to have things back to normal)* Thank
21   you. If we could just get on with the study?
22   MR. MERRIL: Oh, sure. Sorry about all that.
23   RESEARCHER: It's quite all right. OK, "Mother."
24   MR. MERRIL: *(Jumps up in fear.)* Aaaa!
25   RESEARCHER: *(Startled)* What?!
26   MR. MERRIL: *(Jumps on top of chair.)* Get it away from me! Get it
27   away! *(Points to floor.)*
28   RESEARCHER: *(Peers at floor.)* You mean the ant?
29   MR. MERRIL: Yes! Keep it away from me!
30   RESEARCHER: *(Exasperated, stomps on floor.)* There. It's dead.
31   MR. MERRIL: *(Horrified)* You killed it?! How could you?
32   RESEARCHER: *(Stunned)* What?
33   MR. MERRIL: *(Steps off chair, kneels on floor.)* The poor thing! It
34   wasn't going to hurt anybody.
35   RESEARCHER: You just acted like it was going to eat you alive …

1   MR. MERRIL: Don't be ridiculous. You're supposed to be a scientist.
2   RESEARCHER: I don't believe this.
3   MR. MERRIL: We have to have a funeral.
4   RESEARCHER: For an ant?!
5   MR. MERRIL: Everything deserves a Christian burial.
6   RESEARCHER: OK, we'll have a funeral.
7   MR. MERRIL: He needs a coffin.
8   RESEARCHER: You're   joking.   *(MR.   MERRIL   glares   at*
9   *RESEARCHER.)* **Fine.** *(RESEARCHER grabs the box, dumps out*
10   *the pencils.)* **Here, put him in this.**
11 MR. MERRIL: Gross. I'm not picking him up. You do it.
12 RESEARCHER: *(Getting annoyed)* **OK.** *(Pantomimes picking up ant*
13   *and putting it in box. Hands box to MR. MERRIL.)* **Here.**
14 MR. MERRIL: Could you say a few words? *(RESEARCHER stares*
15   *at him in disbelief.)* **Please?**
16 RESEARCHER: *(Resigned to it, if it will end this)* **God? This is an ant.**
17   **It's dead.** *(Looks at MR. MERRIL, who nods encouragingly.)* **I**
18   **killed it. I'm sorry.** *(MR. MERRIL beams happily. RESEARCHER*
19   *is starting to warm up to this.)* **We never really knew this ant …**
20 MR. MERRIL: *(Tosses box aside carelessly.)* **OK, that's enough. It's**
21   **just an ant.** *(He walks back to chair and sits down.)*
22 RESEARCHER: Mr. Merril … *(Pronounces it MER-ril.)*
23 MR. MERRIL: Mer-*ril*.
24 RESEARCHER: I don't think I want to continue with this study.
25 MR. MERRIL: Oh, come on. I'm ready now. I'll control myself.
26 RESEARCHER: No more emotional outbursts?
27 MR. MERRIL: None. I promise. Cross my heart and hope to die.
28 RESEARCHER: I should be so lucky.
29 MR. MERRIL: What was that?
30 RESEARCHER: *(Sits.)* **Nothing. Where were we … ah, there.**
31   *(Looks at MR. MERRIL.)* **"Mother."**
32 MR. MERRIL: *(Leaning forward)* **You have the most beautiful blue**
33   **eyes.**
34 RESEARCHER: *(Slams clipboard on desk.)***That's it! This study is**
35   **over!** *(RESEARCHER stands and starts to leave.)*

1   **MR. MERRIL:** **You're leaving me? But we've only just met ...**
2   **RESEARCHER:** *(Stops and turns to speak.)* **Mr. Mer-*ril*, you need**
3   **serious emotional help. May I encourage you to seek it.** *(MR.*
4   *MERRIL opens his mouth to speak.)* **Elsewhere!** *(RESEARCHER*
5   *exits.)*
6   **MR. MERRIL:** *(Looks after RESEARCHER for a moment, then picks*
7   *up clipboard and pencil, begins writing.)* **Subject "A" reacted**
8   **negatively to strong emotional stimuli, growing extremely**
9   **frustrated as test continued.** *(He puts down the clipboard.)*
10   **Next!**

Surrounded

Synopsis: We watch a man suffering after the loss of his wife, hearing the emotional voices that are overwhelming his soul. In the end he cries out for someone to help, even as the voices drive him into despair. This haunting sketch shows how the emotions of grief come in a random rush, sweeping us along in a turmoil that only God can still.

Theme: Where can we turn for release in our grief?

Topics: Death, grief, loss of a loved one, tragedy

Type: Drama

Cast: 1 man, 4 gender-neutral roles:
MAN — 30s-40s. Grieving for his wife. He has just rushed out of a memorial service, unable to accept what is happening.
FACES 1–4 — Nameless characters, dressed all in black.

Props: None

Set: Bare stage. If possible, the lighting should be dim, except for a central pool of light.

1   *(The four FACES stand in the darkness along the curtain, evenly*
2   *spaced, heads down, unmoving. The MAN enters and walks to*
3   *Downstage Center. The FACES do not acknowledge each other or*
4   *react to the MAN's speech emotionally. Their statements are*
5   *offered flatly and firmly, almost as commands, devoid of any*
6   *emotional tone. The MAN does not acknowledge the FACES at*
7   *all. They represent the thoughts and emotions which are*
8   *overwhelming him, not individuals or even voices that he hears.)*
9   **MAN: I'm sorry, Lisa. I just couldn't stay in there anymore. That**
10   **wasn't you in there. None of that was you. I just had to get**
11   **away. I don't know what everyone must be thinking. But you**
12   **understand, don't you? I just felt surrounded. Ever since this**
13   **happened, I've been feeling surrounded.**
14   **It's just that I don't know how to handle this. This isn't the**
15   **way things were supposed to be. You're supposed to be here.**
16   **With me. Not … I'm not supposed to do this alone. You know**
17   **that, don't you?**
18   **FACE 1:** *(Lifts head.)* **Doubt.** *(Drops head.)*
19   **MAN: Because I'm not sure I *can* do this alone. There's Jenny and**
20   **Allison and Tommy — and I don't know that I'm enough.**
21   **How am I supposed to help them with … with something I**
22   **can't handle myself? They need you. I need you.**
23   **FACE 2:** *(Lifts head.)* **Fear.** *(Drops head.)*
24   **MAN: How are they going to make it? How am I going to make it?**
25   **It's like the whole world is getting dark and …**
26   **FACE 3:** *(Lifts head.)* **Frustration.** *(Drops head.)*
27   **MAN: … I don't know what to do to stop it. It's all rushing so fast**
28   **and I want it all to just stop so that maybe I can try and put**
29   **it all together, to have it make sense …**
30   **FACE 4:** *(Lifts head.)* **Anger.** *(Drops head.)*
31   **MAN: But it won't make sense. Nothing about this has made any**
32   **sense since it started.**
33   **FACE 1:** *(Lifts head.)* **Regret.** *(Drops head.)*
34   **MAN: I keep going over it and over it in my head. I keep thinking**
35   **that I should have been there.**

1   FACE 2: *(Lifts head.)* **Guilt.** *(Drops head.)*

2   MAN: That if only I had left a little quicker, driven a little faster, I

3   could have been there, and then maybe I could have done

4   something, anything — held your hand. I could have ...

5   FACE 3: *(Lifts head.)* **Helplessness.** *(Drops head.)*

6   MAN: ... done nothing. Who am I kidding? There's nothing I

7   could do. Nothing at all. You were surrounded by doctors. I

8   couldn't have done anything but get in the way. If only ...

9   FACE 4: *(Lifts head.)* **Blame.** *(Drops head.)*

10   MAN: ... you hadn't been in that car! I told you I'd pick you up,

11   but you wouldn't listen. How could you have been so stupid!

12   FACE 1: *(Lifts head.)* **Shame.** *(Drops head.)*

13   MAN: I'm sorry. I didn't mean that. I ... I don't know what I mean

14   anymore. I ...

15   FACE 2: *(Lifts head.)* **Confusion.** *(Drops head.)*

16   MAN: ... just don't know what to say, I don't know what to do.

17   And you're not here to help me. You'll never be here to help

18   me again.

19   FACE 3: *(Lifts head.)* **Loss.** *(Drops head.)*

20   MAN: I just want to hold you, Lisa. I just want to hear you say

21   everything will be OK. Because right now, nothing is OK. And

22   I'm afraid nothing will ever be OK again. Oh Lisa, tell me

23   what to do.

24   FACE 4: *(Lifts head.)* **Despair.** *(Drops head.)*

25   MAN: Please, Lisa. Can you hear me, Lisa? Can anybody hear me?

26   *(The FACES move forward as they speak, surrounding the MAN.*

27   *He wilts under their voices.)*

28   FACE 1: Doubt.

29   FACE 2: Fear.

30   FACE 3: Frustration.

31   FACE 4: Anger.

32   FACE 1: Regret.

33   FACE 2: Guilt.

34   FACE 3: Helplessness.

35   FACE 4: Blame.

1   FACE 1: Shame.
2   FACE 2: Confusion.
3   FACE 3: Loss.
4   FACE 4: Despair. *(The FACES now speak simultaneously, a babble of*
5   *noise.)*
6   FACE 1: Doubt. Regret. Shame. *(Repeat)*
7   FACE 2: Fear. Guilt. Confusion. *(Repeat)*
8   FACE 3: Frustration. Helplessness. Loss. *(Repeat)*
9   FACE 4: Anger. Blame. Despair. *(Repeat)*
10   *(MAN wilts under the repetition as the lights, if available, fade to*
11   *black.)*

The System

Synopsis: A young job seeker confesses his secret system for landing employment — total dishonesty — to a stranger in an elevator. The dishonest job seeker gets his just desserts in a surprise ending, revealing the importance of character and integrity in every part of life.

Theme: Character is important in every part of life.

Topics: Character, honesty, integrity, lying, values/morality

Type: Comedy

Cast: 2 men (both roles can be easily adapted for women):
MAN ON AN ELEVATOR
JOB SEEKER

Props: Business card

Set: An elevator in a high-rise office building. (An empty stage is fine.)

1   *(The MAN ON THE ELEVATOR is alone On-stage. He stands as*
2   *if waiting for something [the doors], then steps forward and turns*
3   *to face the audience. He pantomimes pushing a button, then puts*
4   *his hands behind his back and looks up, as if he is looking at the*
5   *numbers over the elevator door. Suddenly the JOB SEEKER runs*
6   *On-stage, waving excitedly.)*
7   **JOB SEEKER: Wait! Hold the door, please!**
8   **MAN:** *(Leans forward and pantomimes pushing a button.)* **Got it.**
9   **JOB SEEKER:** *(Steps into elevator.)* **Thanks. I guess I could have**
10   **waited for it to come back down.**
11 **MAN: Believe me, you don't want to wait for this elevator.**
12 **JOB SEEKER: Slow?**
13 **MAN: Like a Sunday morning sermon.**
14 **JOB SEEKER: Ooo. Glad I got on. I wouldn't want to be late for**
15   **my interview because of an elevator.**
16 **MAN: Oh? Who are you interviewing with?**
17 **JOB SEEKER: Paradise Software. They've got an office on the top**
18   **floor. Have you heard of them?**
19 **MAN: Yes, I've been in their office many times.** *(Pause. JOB*
20   *SEEKER and MAN turn to look up above the "elevator doors."*
21   *Their eyes and heads move as if following the numbers.)*
22 **JOB SEEKER: Actually, I probably wouldn't be late if I had**
23   **waited on the elevator. As a matter of fact, I'm about fifteen**
24   **minutes early. They like it when you're early.**
25 **MAN: Well, I suppose that would be a plus.**
26 **JOB SEEKER: Oh yeah, I've got the timing down to a science. You**
27   **show up early for the interview, and then every day for the**
28   **first six weeks you beat the boss in to work — but the first few**
29   **days you hide out in your office with the door closed until**
30   **about thirty minutes *after* you're officially supposed to arrive.**
31   **So nobody sees you come in, and the boss thinks you're late,**
32   **and then you walk out and surprise him.**
33 **MAN: I see. So he knows you've been there all along. I can see that**
34   **would make an impression.**
35 **JOB SEEKER: Yeah. It makes 'em think you're a real go-getter.**

1   But the best part of it is, once the boss thinks you're there
2   early every day, he won't notice if you come in late. He'll just
3   assume you've been working in your office all morning. Great,
4   isn't it?

5 MAN: I have to admit that's quite a system.

6 JOB SEEKER: Thanks.

7 MAN: But first you've got to land the job.

8 JOB SEEKER: Oh, that's easy.

9 MAN: *(Mildly surprised)* Easy — really?

10 JOB SEEKER: Yeah. Look, interviewers are all alike. They all ask
11   the same dull, boring questions: "Tell me about yourself."
12   "Why do you want to work here?" "Where do you see yourself
13   in ten years?" I've never met an interviewer who had an
14   original question.

15 MAN: But you still have to answer those questions …

16 JOB SEEKER: Yeah, but it's like being given a copy of the exam
17   two weeks beforehand — even better, because the
18   interviewers don't even know what answers they really want.
19   You just kiss up to 'em, talk about "vision" and "goals,"
20   appeal to the old corporate ego, and you're in.

21 MAN: Surely it's not as easy as that. You've got to demonstrate
22   your knowledge and experience.

23 JOB SEEKER: Ha! That's the easiest part of all — you don't need
24   any! *(Conspiratorially)* You just lie!

25 MAN: *(Pretending shock)* No!

26 JOB SEEKER: Yes! Just like this: *(In a deeper "professional" tone)*
27   "Why yes, in my previous position I oversaw a staff of twenty-
28   five market strategists and support personnel. Under my
29   leadership we increased our market share by fifteen percent in
30   less than two years."

31 MAN: But when they check your references, they'll find out it's not
32   true.

33 JOB SEEKER: That's what's so great — they almost never check
34   your references. They actually take you at your word. Can you
35   believe it?

1   MAN: *(Dryly)* **Incredible.**

2   JOB SEEKER: **And even if they do check, I've got that covered.**

3   **All my references are fakes.**

4   MAN: **Oh, come on. They'll see through that the minute they get a**

5   **wrong number.**

6   JOB SEEKER: **Ah, but they won't get a wrong number. They'll get**

7   **two old frat brothers of mine and a cousin in Phoenix. We've**

8   **all worked it out together. Whenever one of us has an**

9   **interview, we back each other up. It's perfect!**

10   MAN: **I guess your system is perfect, except for one thing — Ah,**

11   **here's my floor.** *(He starts to step out of the "elevator.")*

12   JOB SEEKER: **What's that?**

13   MAN: *(Hands him a business card.)* **You should be more careful who**

14   **you talk to in elevators.**

15   JOB SEEKER: *(Reads card aloud.)* **"Scott Markham, President,**

16   **Paradise Software."**

17   MAN: **I suggest you just press the button for "lobby." Enjoy the**

18   **ride down.** *(MAN exits. JOB SEEKER just stares at the card.)*

T.G.I.F.

Synopsis: The sketch opens on Monday morning, as two men slave away at jobs they obviously despise, ruining their health and living in pure misery. They have dreams of doing something else — one photography, the other cooking — but they think these activities are to be saved for Friday. But when Friday finally comes, we discover our harried workers have put off their dreams one day too many.

Theme: When should we pursue our dreams?

Topics: Dreams, fulfillment, goals, God's purpose for us, money/materialism, stress, success, talents, trusting God, work

Type: Comedy

Cast: 2 men:
BILLY WORKMAN — Stressed-out accountant. Dreams of being a photographer.
LARRY JONES — Stressed-out accountant. Dreams of being a chef.

Props: A large flip chart "calendar." Top page reads "Monday," next page reads "Wednesday," and last page reads "Friday"; two noisy adding machines; a pill bottle with pills inside; a photograph; a piece of Tupperware or similar container; a spoon; a camera; a wok; a small cooler; sunglasses; sunscreen; a loud Hawaiian shirt; two briefcases

Set: A nondescript office, with two identical desks side by side and two chairs. Adding machines are on the desks. There's a photo on one desk and a Tupperware container on the other. The calendar is located at Upstage Center, midway between the two desks so that the actors can easily reach it. The date reads "Monday." The wok, cooler, sunscreen, camera and Hawaiian shirt are hidden from the audience's view but are easily accessible to the actors.

1   *(BILLY and LARRY enter carrying briefcases, walking the same*
2   *way, very rapidly. Each has on a white collared shirt, loose tie*
3   *and dark slacks. Both are harried, agitated and stressed-out*
4   *beyond belief. They sit down simultaneously and start pounding*
5   *furiously on their adding machines. Their conversation is rapid-*
6   *fire, almost a fever pitch.)*
7   **BILLY:** *(Stressed)* **Morning, Larry.**
8   **LARRY:** *(Equally stressed)* **Morning, Billy.**
9   **BILLY: Looks like another Monday.**
10   **LARRY: All day long.**
11   **BILLY: Yep. But cheer up, Friday's coming!**
12   **LARRY: T.G.I.F.!**
13   **BILLY: T.G.I.F.!**
14   **LARRY: Hoo boy!**
15   **BILLY: But today it's Monday.**
16   **LARRY: Daily grind.**
17   **BILLY: Nose to the grindstone.**
18   **LARRY: Work, work, work.** *(They pound furiously on their adding*
19   *machines, typing and totaling in perfect sync. They even pause to*
20   *look at the tape at the same time in the exact same way. This*
21   *should be rapid-fire and very rhythmical: pound, pound, total —*
22   *lift up tape; pound, pound, total — lift up tape. This action*
23   *repeats twice. On the third time, both stop simultaneously and rub*
24   *their left arms in exactly the same way. Throughout this sequence,*
25   *neither is aware that their actions are identical. BILLY takes the*
26   *pill bottle out of his shirt pocket, pours out a pill, and offers the*
27   *bottle to LARRY, while rapidly shaking it in a nervous twitch.)*
28   **BILLY: Stresstab?**
29   **LARRY: Thanks.** *(They swallow the pills, LARRY swallowing straight*
30   *from the bottle. He hands it back. They return to pounding on the*
31   *adding machines.)*
32   **BILLY: You don't look so good, Larry.**
33   **LARRY: You look flat awful, Billy.**
34   **BILLY: Yeah. The wife wants me to see a doctor.**
35   **LARRY: Mine too.**

1   BILLY: You going to?

2   LARRY: I might. When I can find a free day.

3   BILLY: Yeah. Me too.

4   LARRY: But it won't be Friday!

5   BILLY: Not gonna give up Friday, not to a doctor!

6   LARRY: T.G.I.F.!

7   BILLY: T.G.I.F.!

8   LARRY: Hoo boy!

9   BILLY: You got those figures for the Grierson account?

10 LARRY: What?

11 BILLY: The figures for the Grierson account — you got 'em?

12 LARRY: Gruesome Grierson?

13 BILLY: That's the one.

14 LARRY: Not yet. But I'll have them on Wednesday. *(If possible, lights*

15   *blackout. They reach over together and flip the calendar page. It*

16   *now reads Wednesday. Lights up. They're still pounding away.)*

17 BILLY: *(Still as stressed as ever)* Wednesday.

18 LARRY: *(Ditto)* Over-the-hump day!

19 BILLY: Halfway to Friday!

20 LARRY: T.G.I.F.!

21 BILLY: T.G.I.F.!

22 LARRY: Hoo boy!

23 BILLY: But today it's Wednesday.

24 LARRY: All day!

25 BILLY: Got those Grierson figures?

26 LARRY: Gruesome Grierson?

27 BILLY: Grimy Gruesome Grierson.

28 LARRY: Here you go.

29 BILLY: Thanks.

30 LARRY: Say, what are you going to do?

31 BILLY: I'm going to finish the Grierson account.

32 LARRY: No, I mean on Friday.

33 BILLY: *(Stops pounding, looks wistfully into the distance.)* Friday …

34   I'm going to take pictures.

35 LARRY: Pictures?

1	**BILLY:** *(Eager, can't wait to do this)* **Yeah. Sweeping panoramas,**
2	**close-up details, studies of light and shadow.**
3	**LARRY: Wow. You're really into it.**
4	**BILLY: Yeah. Here, look at this one.** *(Picks up a photograph and*
5	*hands it to LARRY.)*
6	**LARRY: Wow. That's some photo. Did you take this?**
7	**BILLY: Yep. On a Friday.**
8	**LARRY: Good day for it.**
9	**BILLY: Great day for it.**
10	**LARRY: T.G.I.F.!**
11	**BILLY: T.G.I.F.!**
12	**LARRY: Hoo boy!** *(They go back to pounding in unison on their*
13	*adding machines.)*
14	**BILLY: So how about you?**
15	**LARRY: Huh?**
16	**BILLY: What are you gonna do on Friday?**
17	**LARRY: I don't know. I'll probably cook.**
18	**BILLY: You cook?**
19	**LARRY:** *(Enthusiastic about it)* **I love to cook.**
20	**BILLY: Any good?**
21	**LARRY: Taste this.** *(He pulls out the Tupperware bowl, sticks a spoon*
22	*in and hands the spoon to BILLY.)*
23	**BILLY:** *(Eats furiously.)* **Mmmm.** *(Eats more.)*
24	**LARRY: What did I tell you?**
25	**BILLY:** *(Almost with his mouth full)* **You ever thought about just**
26	**doing this?**
27	**LARRY: Cooking?**
28	**BILLY: Yeah. There's good money in cooking.**
29	**LARRY: But it's risky.**
30	**BILLY: Big-time risky.** *(They return to pounding.)*
31	**LARRY: Like photography.**
32	**BILLY: Yeah.**
33	**LARRY: But I can always do it on Friday!**
34	**BILLY: T.G.I.F.!**
35	**LARRY: T.G.I.F.!** *(Suddenly they rub their left arms, simultaneously.)*

171

1   BILLY: Need to see that doctor.
2   LARRY: Yep. Maybe make an appointment for Monday.
3   BILLY: Yeah. Monday. *(If possible, lights blackout. They reach over*
4   *together and flip the calendar page. It now reads Friday.)*
5   BILLY: *(Excited)* **It's Friday!**
6   LARRY: *(Jumps up, excited. Holds up a wok.)* **I've got my wok!**
7   BILLY: *(Jumps up, holds up a camera.)* **I've got my camera!**
8   LARRY: *(Holds up a cooler.)* **I've got my cooler!**
9   BILLY: *(Puts sunscreen on nose.)* **I've got my sunscreen!**
10 LARRY: *(Puts on sunglasses.)* **I've got my cool shades!**
11 BILLY: *(Pulls Hawaiian shirt over his work shirt.)* **I've got my loud**
12   **Hawaiian shirt!**
13 LARRY: *(Can't top this, holds up wok again.)* **I've got my wok!**
14 BILLY: **T.G.I.F!**
15 LARRY: **T.G.I.F.!**
16 TOGETHER: *(They "high five" each other with their right hands.)*
17   **Thank God It's ...** *(Suddenly they come down out of the "high*
18   *five" to rub their left arms, and immediately both clutch their chests*
19   *in the same way.)* **Hoooo boy!** *(They collapse on their desks.)*

True Believer

Synopsis: A young woman's dependence on a psychic hotline leads to her ruin when the charlatan on the phone and her unbelieving boyfriend conspire to swindle her fortune. This sketch offers an excellent depiction of how misplaced faith can have disastrous consequences. *Note: "True Believer" runs 8 to 10 minutes. This sketch can be divided into three 3-minute acts for added dramatic impact.*

Theme: Where can we find real help and real hope?

Topics: A lost world, false gods, false religion, New Age, psychic hotlines

Type: Drama

Cast: 2 men, 1 woman:
"SWAMI RAMIL AMA DEEN GADONG" / RANDY
    DEAN — A phone psychic
MARIANNE WELLS — A young woman, a patron of the
    Swami (She'll need an extra sweater or other clothing item)
DAMIAN — A blind date/ Marianne's boyfriend, tall and
    handsome (he'll also need a new shirt or other
    clothing item)

Props: Two phones, caller ID screen, adding machine, snack in a bag, earrings and other jewelry, picnic basket, bill of sale

Set: The stage is divided into two areas: The SWAMI's office, with a desk, chair, phone, and adding machine. A Caller ID device is attached to the phone (if one is not available, fake it). The other side of the stage is Marianne's apartment, with two chairs (or a sofa), a coffee table and a phone.

Sound Effects: Off-stage voice or taped recording for answering machine message.

1   *(SWAMI RAMIL is sitting at his desk with his feet propped on the*
2   *desk. The SWAMI is an ordinary American guy, with nothing special*
3   *or exotic about his clothing or appearance. He is eating a snack,*
4   *tossing the pieces into the air and trying to catch them with his*
5   *mouth. MARIANNE is in her apartment. She is just finishing getting*
6   *dressed, putting on earrings and jewelry as if she is about to go out*
7   *on a date. She is clearly nervous. She looks at the phone and on an*
8   *impulse, picks it up and dials. The phone in the SWAMI's office rings,*
9   *but he does not answer. Instead, an answering machine picks up. The*
10   *SWAMI mouths along with the message while gazing at his watch.)*
11 **ANSWERING MACHINE: Salutations, oh true believer! You have**
12   **reached the Psychic Wisdom Alliance, where we will unfold**
13   **the mysteries of the past and future to you, all for only four**
14   **dollars and ninety-nine cents a minute. All of our psychic**
15   **counselors are currently ministering to other callers. Please**
16   **stay on the line. We know how important your call is, and a**
17   **psychic counselor will be with you as soon as possible.** *(New*
18   *Age hold music begins to play. The SWAMI does not pick up the*
19   *phone, but continues to stare at his watch. MARIANNE nods her*
20   *head to the music, then starts to put down the phone. Just as she*
21   *pulls it away from her ear, the SWAMI picks up his phone.)*
22 **SWAMI:** *(He speaks with a fake exotic Asian accent.)* **Hello, true believer!**
23   **This is the Swami Ramil Ama Deen Gadong. Please do not speak,**
24   **but listen to me very carefully.** *(MARIANNE follows his*
25   *instructions.)* **Close your eyes and slowly let your breath out,**
26   **cleansing your mind of all foreign thoughts ... Ahh ... Yes, I can**
27   **feel your spirit.** *(MARIANNE opens her mouth to speak, but stops.)*
28   **Do not tell me your name. It is written within you for me to read.**
29   *(He holds up the Caller ID device and reads it.)* **Mar ... Mary ...**
30   **Marianne ...** *(MARIANNE looks surprised and pleased.)* **Wait, there**
31   **is more ... I see deep water, a dark place ... a well?** *(As if he has*
32   *come to recognition)* **Marianne Wells! Hello again, Miss Marianne!**
33 **MARIANNE:** *(Delighted)* **Oh, Swami, how do you do that? Every**
34   **time I call, you know who it is and I don't even have to say**
35   **anything!**

1   SWAMI: Ah, but your mind is like a clear pool to me, Miss
2   Marianne. But I can tell something is troubling the waters ...
3   a man ... a stranger?
4   MARIANNE: *(Excited)* Yes, yes! Someone responded to my
5   personal ad, and we're meeting for the first time tonight. Oh,
6   Swami, is this the right man for me?
7   SWAMI: What you ask is very difficult. Please, I must concentrate
8   for a moment. *(He puts down the phone and calmly eats some more*
9   *of his snack. MARIANNE waits in anticipation. He picks the phone*
10   *back up.)* Ah, yes, I see him. He is tall, handsome — he walks
11   with confidence, a man of business, but filled with a heart that
12   is searching for love. His search is for you, Miss Marianne.
13   MARIANNE: *(Delighted)* Oh Swami, that sounds wonderful! I can
14   see him through the window now! *(DAMIAN enters.)* He is
15   handsome! And tall! Swami, I don't know how to thank you!
16   SWAMI: Your continued happiness is sufficient, Miss Marianne.
17   *(They both hang up. MARIANNE and DAMIAN greet, kiss each*
18   *other on the cheek and exit. At the same time the SWAMI looks at*
19   *his watch and punches some numbers on the adding machine. He*
20   *looks at the tape. Then, with no accent)* That, and your limitless
21   bank account.
22
23   *(MARIANNE and DAMIAN reenter, their clothing altered enough to*
24   *hint that this is not the same night. She is carrying a picnic basket.)*
25   MARIANNE: Damian, that was a wonderful picnic. I wish you
26   could stay longer today.
27   DAMIAN: So do I, Marianne, but this appointment can't wait.
28   This deal is the breakthrough I've been struggling for.
29   MARIANNE: *(Timidly)* Damian, I know you don't like me to bring
30   this up ...
31   DAMIAN: Yes?
32   MARIANNE: *(In a rush)* But won't you call the Swami, just this
33   once — he could help you see how the meeting is going to be,
34   maybe even help you prepare for it ...
35   DAMIAN: *(Firmly)* No, Marianne. You know how I feel about those

1   psychic hotlines. He's a charlatan, Marianne.

2   MARIANNE: No, he really does know what's going to happen! He

3   told me about you.

4   DAMIAN: I know, "tall and handsome, a businessman." There

5   must be thousands of men in this city who meet that

6   description. Your "Swami" just made a safe guess and got

7   lucky. I don't like you wasting your money on this guy.

8   MARIANNE: Damian, I'm sure he really did see you. And it's not

9   just that, he tells me so much about myself. Anyway, I'm not

10   in danger of going broke.

11   DAMIAN: *(More tenderly)* Marianne, I just don't want to see you

12   get hurt. You've come to mean so much to me in these last few

13   weeks, I ... *(He stumbles on the words, then looks at his watch.)*

14   I have to go. But Marianne, we'll have a lot to talk about when

15   I get back. I love you. *(They kiss and he exits. She immediately*

16   *picks up the phone and dials. The SWAMI's phone rings, and he*

17   *picks it up.)*

18   SWAMI: Hello, true believer! This is the Swami Ramil Ama Deen

19   Gadong. Please do not speak ...

20   MARIANNE: *(Interrupts excitedly.)* Swami, it's me, Marianne!

21   SWAMI: Miss Marianne! How nice to be talking to you again. But

22   please, you break my concentration when you speak up like

23   that.

24   MARIANNE: I know, Swami, but I was just so excited I had to call

25   you.

26   SWAMI: Yes, I can see that your waters are swirling rapidly. It is

27   your friend Damian, is it not?

28   MARIANNE: Yes, it's Damian — I think he's going to ask me to

29   marry him!

30   SWAMI: Oh, how delightful for you, Miss Marianne! But what

31   then is your question for your humble Swami?

32   MARIANNE: Swami, tell me how our life will be — what do you

33   see?

34   SWAMI: You ask much, Miss Marianne, many years through

35   which I must peer, through waters unfathomed. Please, I must

1   concentrate. *(He puts down the phone, stretches, cracks his*
2   *knuckles and picks the phone back up.)* **I see warm waters, deep**
3   **and endless — a happy life, yes? But the waters part. One way**
4   **is warm and deep, but down the other lies darkness.**
5   **MARIANNE:** *(Worried)* **What does that mean, Swami?**
6   **SWAMI: Something touches Damian. Around him are whirlpools**
7   **that would drag him down into the dark waters. You must**
8   **save him, Miss Marianne, for his own happiness and yours. I**
9   **cannot see more.**
10   **MARIANNE: Thank you, Swami. I will do whatever I must. Good-**
11   **bye, Swami.**
12   **SWAMI: Many blessings, Miss Marianne.** *(They hang up. DAMIAN*
13   *enters. He looks defeated.)*
14   **MARIANNE: Damian! I didn't expect you back so soon.**
15   **DAMIAN: Neither did I.**
16   **MARIANNE:** *(Worried)* **What's wrong?**
17   **DAMIAN: I got a call on my cell phone. One of the investors pulled**
18   **out. He was our biggest source of capital. The other investors**
19   **just don't have the resources to make up the difference. If we**
20   **can't find another investor, the deal's a complete bust.**
21   **MARIANNE:** *(To herself)* **Dark waters …**
22   **DAMIAN:** *(Despairing)* **Marianne, I don't know what I'm going to**
23   **do. I had everything poured into this — I've already placed**
24   **orders for the heavy equipment.** *(He pulls out a bill of sale and*
25   *puts it on the coffee table. MARIANNE picks it up.)* **My suppliers**
26   **expect payment on arrival. Marianne, this could break me.**
27   **MARIANNE:** *(Resolved)* **Don't worry, Damian, you've got a third**
28   **investor.**
29   **DAMIAN: What are you talking about?**
30   **MARIANNE: I'm talking about me.**
31   **DAMIAN: Marianne, don't joke about this. You don't have that**
32   **kind of money.**
33   **MARIANNE: Yes, I do. My father left me more than enough to**
34   **meet this** *(She waves the bill)* **and back your project as well.**
35   *(She writes something on the back of the bill.)* **Here, take this to**

1   **Chase Manhattan. They'll transfer all the funds you need.**

2   *(She gives the paper to DAMIAN.)*

3   **DAMIAN:** **Marianne, I can't take this.**

4   **MARIANNE:** **Yes, you can. Don't argue with me, Damian. I'm just**

5   **making sure the waters will be warm.**

6   **DAMIAN:** **I don't know what you mean by that, but it doesn't**

7   **matter. Marianne, I love you.**

8   **MARIANNE:** *(They embrace, then she pulls away.)* **Go. I'll wait for**

9   **you.** *(DAMIAN leaves her area. She looks after him, then exits in*

10   *the opposite direction. DAMIAN crosses to the SWAMI's office.*

11   *The SWAMI is on the phone.)*

12   **DAMIAN:** *(Enters the office.)* **You got the tickets?**

13   **SWAMI:** **I'm confirming them right now.** *(In phone)* **Yes, Flight 279,**

14   **First Class. Good. We'll be there.** *(To DAMIAN)* **Did you get**

15   **the cash?**

16   **DAMIAN:** **Wired and on its way.**

17   **SWAMI:** **Wahoo, we're off to Rio!**

18   **DAMIAN:** **After you, Swami.** *(They leave. The phone rings and the*

19   *answering machine picks up.)*

20   **ANSWERING MACHINE:** **Salutations, oh true believer!**

What's the Word?

Synopsis: A woman expects that her new boyfriend's "important question" will be the "big one." It's coming a little too soon for her, so she turns to her girlfriends for advice. When the boyfriend arrives in the middle of the discussion, the confusion grows. His words (a desire for companionship, accepting new responsibilities) play into her assumptions — until he pops the question: What kind of dog should he get? Elation turns to deflation, and everyone leaves disappointed — especially the boyfriend, who has no idea what he said wrong.

Theme: Why is it so hard to say the right thing?

Topics: Communication, dating, miscommunication, the power of words, relationships, saying the right thing/saying the wrong thing

Type: Comedy

Cast: 3 women, 1 man:
JANIE — A young woman worried about a big decision
BONNIE — Janie's friend
CAROL — Janie's friend
RICHARD — Janie's boyfriend

Props: None

Set: A restaurant — table, tablecloth, four chairs, menus, water glasses and a centerpiece.

1   *(BONNIE and CAROL are sitting at the table, looking around.*
2   *JANIE enters, gazing around, as if looking for someone.)*
3   **CAROL:** *(Spotting JANIE)* **There she is.** *(Calls.)* **Janie!**
4   **JANIE:** *(Walks quickly to them. A little nervous)* **Bonnie, Carol.**
5   **Thanks for meeting me here!**
6   **BONNIE: So, what's the word? Why'd you call this con-flab?**
7   **JANIE: It's Richard. I'm supposed to meet him here in about**
8   **twenty minutes.**
9   **CAROL: And ... ?**
10   **JANIE: He said he wanted to ask me something important.**
11   *(BONNIE and CAROL react with excitement.)*
12   **CAROL: Oooo! This is so terrific!**
13   **JANIE: No!**
14   **BONNIE:** *(Taken aback)* **It's not terrific?**
15   **JANIE: No! I mean yes, I mean ... I don't know! I'm just not**
16   **ready!**
17   **CAROL: Honey, if our *waiter* asked me, I'd be ready.**
18   **BONNIE: Me too. I've seen our waiter!**
19   **JANIE: Guys! This is serious!**
20   **CAROL: OK, Janie, do you want to get married?**
21   **JANIE: No! Well, yes. Eventually.**
22   **BONNIE: Do you want to get married to Richard?**
23   **JANIE: I don't know! We've only been dating for a couple of months.**
24   **CAROL: So he moves fast. You could do worse in a guy.**
25   **BONNIE: Now hold on, Carol. If you ask me, a guy who pops the**
26   **question this quickly is risky territory. Any guy should think**
27   **twice before asking Janie to marry him.**
28   **JANIE: Gee, thanks.**
29   **BONNIE: That's not what I meant. You just don't want to be**
30   **hooked up with the kind of guy who rushes into things.**
31   **CAROL: Unless he looks like our waiter.**
32   **BONNIE: Amen, sister!** *(BONNIE and CAROL high five.)*
33   **JANIE: Guys! Help me out here! Richard is going to be here soon,**
34   **and I don't know what to say!**
35   **BONNIE: Give it to him straight, girl. Tell him it's a dumb idea.**

1   You know what I say — "Honesty is the best policy."

2   CAROL: Were you being honest when you told Sarah Moore she'd

3   look good with bronze hair?

4   BONNIE: I meant highlights! I didn't think she'd turn herself into

5   a lawn ornament.

6   JANIE: Too metallic?

7   BONNIE: The girl's head attracts lightning.

8   CAROL: Look, Janie, forget the honesty stuff. Nobody wants to

9   hear what you really think. Especially men.

10   JANIE: You're saying I should lie to him?

11   CAROL: No, not lie — just tell him what he wants to hear.

12   JANIE: What he wants to hear, I can't say! At least not yet!

13   CAROL: So you're just going to shoot him down?

14   BONNIE: That's it, sister! Take aim and *Ka-pow!*

15   JANIE: I don't want to shoot him down! I just want him to think

16   about it carefully.

17   BONNIE: He's already shown he doesn't do that by asking you to

18   marry him.

19   JANIE: You are really boosting my self-esteem.

20   BONNIE: Hey, what are girlfriends for?

21   JANIE: C'mon, guys, what do I say to Richard? *(RICHARD enters*

22   *behind JANIE.)*

23   CAROL: *(Looking past JANIE at RICHARD)* I don't know, but

24   you'd better think of it quick!

25   JANIE: What?

26   RICHARD: *(Spotting them)* Janie?

27   JANIE: *(Turns, caught off guard.)* Richard! You're here! I mean ...

28   you're here early!

29   RICHARD: Yeah. I called your office, and they said you'd already

30   left. I thought maybe I had the time wrong, so I came on over.

31   Hi Bonnie, Carol.

32   BONNIE and CAROL: *(Knowingly)* Hi, Richard.

33   RICHARD: Am I interrupting something?

34   JANIE: *(Too quickly)* No! *(Composing herself, then quickly)* No. I, uh,

35   had a few errands to run before lunch, but I got through early,

1   so here I am. Bonnie and Carol just happened to be here.
2   Right, girls?
3   CAROL: Right.
4   BONNIE: Sure thing.
5   CAROL: This is our favorite restaurant.
6   RICHARD: Oh? What do you like here?
7   BONNIE: The waiter.
8   JANIE: But they were just leaving. Weren't you?
9   CAROL: Right! Gotta go!
10 BONNIE: Say good-bye to the waiter for us!
11 RICHARD: No, that's OK, stick around. You can help us decide.
12 JANIE: They can?
13 RICHARD: *(To JANIE)* Well, they're your best friends. If you trust
14   them, I trust them.
15 CAROL: Richard, I don't really know that we should be a part of
16   this ...
17 RICHARD: Why not? This is a big decision. I'd appreciate your
18   input.
19 JANIE: Richard, maybe we'd better talk about this in private.
20 RICHARD: Why? It's not like it's going to be a secret. Besides,
21   they could help pick out everything we'll need.
22 BONNIE: You do move fast.
23 RICHARD: No use wasting time. If you're going to do something,
24   go ahead and do it. Right, Janie?
25 JANIE: Look, Richard, this is a really big decision. This is a big step.
26 RICHARD: I know. It's going to mean a lot of changes. I'm taking
27   on a new responsibility. I'll have to cut down on business trips,
28   get home from work earlier. And then there's my apartment
29   — it's barely big enough for me as it is. So I guess it's house-
30   hunting time.
31 JANIE: This is a lot to handle at one time.
32 RICHARD: *(Takes her hand.)* I know, Janie. But I finally decided
33   that the love and companionship are worth it. You only go
34   through life once — if something is going to bring you
35   happiness, you need to do it, right?

1   **JANIE:** *(A brief pause, then quietly, deciding.)* **Yes.** *(BONNIE and*
2   *CAROL gasp.)*
3   **RICHARD:** *(Slightly puzzled)* **Yes?**
4   **JANIE:** *(Excitedly)* **Yes! Let's do it, Richard!**
5   **RICHARD: Great! So what do you think, bulldog or golden**
6   **retriever?**
7   **JANIE:** *(Stunned)* **What?**
8   **RICHARD: It's the only thing I'm stuck on. If you're going to get**
9   **a dog, you should choose the right kind. I'm down to bulldog**
10   **or golden retriever.**
11   **JANIE:** *(Still stunned)* **Bulldog or golden …**
12   **RICHARD: Yeah. I know they're kind of extremes. Bulldogs are**
13   **short and squat and kind of ugly, but goldens need more**
14   **room, and you can't exactly name one "Churchill" — it just**
15   **doesn't fit. So, bulldog or golden retriever?** *(To BONNIE and*
16   *CAROL)* **What do you guys think?**
17   **JANIE:** *(Angry, boils over.)* **Oooo! I can't believe you!** *(She storms off.)*
18   **BONNIE:** *(Quickly follows her.)* **Janie! Let me introduce you to our**
19   **waiter!**
20   **CAROL:** *(To RICHARD)* **Men! You never say the right thing!** *(She*
21   *stomps off.)*
22   **RICHARD:** *(Bewildered)* **Uh … beagle?** *(He sits, looking puzzled, as*
23   *the lights, if available, fade to black.)*

Worst-Case Scenario

Synopsis: A young couple anticipates the results of a home pregnancy test. While they wait on a kitchen timer to ring, the husband concocts an ever-more disastrous scenario for their future as parents of a daughter (his "worst-case scenario"). What should be a happy event becomes a threat of impending doom — until the timer dings and the results are known.

Theme: Why do we allow fear to dim our joy?

Topics: False fears, fear of the future, God's control, God's power, parenthood, pregnancy, trusting God

Type: Comedy

Cast: 1 man, 1 woman:
LAURA — Young wife
RICHARD — Young husband, nervous and uptight

Props: Mechanical kitchen timer, pregnancy test kit

Set: The couple's living room, with a sofa and a coffee table. A kitchen timer and a pregnancy kit are on the table.

Sound Effects: Rapid ticking, ding (as if from the timer)

1   *(LAURA sits on the sofa, staring at the timer. RICHARD paces*
2   *nervously. The sound of rapid ticking is heard. It fades out as*
3   *RICHARD begins speaking.)*
4   **RICHARD:** *(Nervous)* **So when will we know?**
5   **LAURA:** *(Nervous, but trying to be calm and collected)* **It takes five**
6   **minutes.**
7   **RICHARD: Couldn't we have gotten something quicker?**
8   **LAURA: Doctor Mason said this was the most accurate one on the**
9   **market.**
10   **RICHARD: Well, it ought to be. Five minutes for something like**
11   **this is an eternity. Don't they have a ten-second test?**
12   **LAURA: What do you want, a countdown? Relax. We'll know**
13   **when we know.**
14   **RICHARD: But we need time to prepare.**
15   **LAURA: Richard, we're going to have nine months.**
16   **RICHARD: That's not enough time. There's just too much at**
17   **stake. This little girl is going to be a real challenge in our lives.**
18   **LAURA: Little girl? That's so sweet. I thought you'd want a boy.**
19   **RICHARD: I'm just thinking of the worst-case scenario.** *(LAURA*
20   *reacts with an odd look, but RICHARD continues without*
21   *noticing.)* **Laura, I don't know anything about little girls. I**
22   **didn't grow up around girls. All my friends were boys. Both**
23   **my brothers were boys.**
24   **LAURA:** *(Appearing confident)* **Well, I think I know plenty about**
25   **little girls.**
26   **RICHARD: What could you know, Laura? You were an only child.**
27   **Face it, Laura, we just aren't prepared for everything this**
28   **baby will mean.**
29   **LAURA: Like diapers and two a.m. feedings? I feel confident we'll**
30   **both rise to the occasion.** *(Thinks about it.)* **Probably**
31   **frequently.**
32   **RICHARD: That's not what I'm talking about, Laura. I'm looking**
33   **at the Big Picture, the perils down the road. This is not the**
34   **happy-go-lucky event you think it is.**
35   **LAURA: Of course it's happy. What perils down the road could**

1   there possibly be?

2   RICHARD: Well, financial problems, for one thing. She's going to

3   need clothes and hair bows and little pink shoes with Sesame

4   Street characters on them ...

5   LAURA: You forgot those cute little dresses with the lace and

6   smocking. *(Dreamily)* I love smocking. All those little folds and

7   crinkles, all bunched in together ...

8   RICHARD: *(Interrupting)* Laura! Would you please focus? I'm in a

9   financial panic here! The last thing I want to hear about is

10   smocking!

11   LAURA: Sorry.

12   RICHARD: It's just another thing on the list of expenses. And what

13   happens when she gets a little older? We've got birthdays and

14   Christmas to worry about. She's going to want Holiday

15   Celebration Barbie dolls and Beanie Babies and Furbys. *(Note*

16   *to director: Feel free to insert the latest obnoxious toy craze in*

17   *place of "Furbys." They both shudder.)* I'm telling you, the older

18   she gets, the more expensive she gets. What about braces and

19   makeup and jewelry? And then there's ballet classes.

20   LAURA: Ballet? What about sports? Just because she's a girl

21   doesn't mean she can't play soccer or baseball!

22   RICHARD: Sports! That's even worse. She could break an arm or

23   a leg!

24   LAURA: *(She doesn't like the sound of that, and decides to be*

25   *protective.)* Break a leg? OK, ballet it is. Or chess. That's nice

26   and safe, isn't it?

27   RICHARD: It won't help. Even if she stays healthy, she'll still

28   become a teenager.

29   LAURA: Ewww.

30   RICHARD: What happens when she gets her driver's license and

31   becomes another menace on the highway?

32   LAURA: Well, hopefully she'll take after her mother.

33   RICHARD: That's what I'm worried about. *(Beat)* But it's not just

34   the driving. What if she turns out to be one of the rebellious

35   ones? What if she wants a nose ring?

1　LAURA: *(Unconcerned)* **Every girl needs a little self-expression.**

2　RICHARD: **OK, what if she dyes her hair green?**

3　LAURA: *(A little less sure, but keeping an open mind)* **She'll grow out**

4　　**of it. Hair color washes out, you know.**

5　RICHARD: *(He leans close to LAURA — he knows he's got her on*

6　　*this one.)* **What if she gets a tattoo.**

7　LAURA: *(Jumping up, adamant)* **Over my dead body!**

8　RICHARD: **I'm telling you, it's going to be nose rings, green hair,**

9　　**and tattoos all the way.**

10　LAURA: **Oh, no it won't. I won't stand for it.**

11　RICHARD: **Doesn't matter. If it's not her, it will be her boyfriend.**

12　LAURA: **Don't be silly. She won't go for a guy like that.**

13　RICHARD: **Oh, yes she will; she'll think he's a *challenge*.**

14　LAURA: *(Horrified)* **Oh, no. She'll *marry* him.**

15　RICHARD: **Uh-huh. And then they'll move in with us, because no**

16　　**way is a guy like that going to be able to find a decent job so**

17　　**he can take care of his family. We'll be paying for everything.**

18　LAURA: **I'll have to get a job!**

19　RICHARD: **More like two. And all the while, that worthless, no-**

20　　**good husband of hers will be lying around the house watching**

21　　**professional wrestling all day, stuffing his face with pork rinds**

22　　**and plotting to steal our retirement.**

23　LAURA: **He wouldn't dare!**

24　RICHARD: **Oh, yes he would — face it, that money is *gone!***

25　LAURA: **She'll stop him.**

26　RICHARD: **No, she won't. She *loves* him. He can do no wrong;**

27　　**we're just her *parents*.**

28　LAURA: **Why, that ungrateful little — after all we've done for**

29　　**her?!**

30　RICHARD: **That's children for you. Nothing but misery all the**

31　　**way.** *(Pause, then timer dings. RICHARD and LAURA pause for*

32　　*a moment. Finally LAURA reaches beside the timer and picks up*

33　　*the kit. She looks at it and turns to RICHARD.)*

34　RICHARD: **What does it say?**

35　LAURA: **It says yes. We're having a baby!** *(They embrace.)*

1   **RICHARD: I've never been so happy in all my life.**
2   **LAURA: Me, too!** *(Brightly, excited)* **What if they're twins?**
3   *(RICHARD reacts with horror. They freeze.)*

Topic Index

189

About the Author

Howard Shirley is a professional writer whose credits include feature articles, devotional guides and Christian devotional videos. Howard began writing short sketches for Bellevue Community Church in Nashville, Tennessee in 1996. Howard served as Bellevue Community Church's chief scriptwriter from 1997 to 2002, and as the drama team leader from 1998 to 2001, and again as drama team co-leader in 2004. Howard lives in Franklin, Tennessee with his wife and son. You may contact Howard by e-mail at actsforgod@aol.com.

Order Form

Meriwether Publishing Ltd.
PO Box 7710
Colorado Springs CO 80933-7710
Phone: 800-937-5297 Fax: 719-594-9916
Website: www.meriwether.com

Please send me the following books:

_____ **Acts for God #BK-B274** $15.95
by Howard Shirley
38 dramatic sketches for contemporary services

_____ **Worship Sketches 2 Perform #BK-B242** $15.95
by Steven James
A collection of scripts for two actors

_____ **More Worship Sketches 2 Perform #BK-B258** $14.95
by Steven James
A collection of scripts for two actors

_____ **Service with a Smile #BK-B225** $14.95
by Daniel Wray
52 humorous sketches for Sunday worship

_____ **More Service with a Smile #BK-B266** $15.95
by Daniel Wray
Another helping of humorous sketches for Sunday worship

_____ **Isaac Air Freight: The Works #BK-B215** $16.95
by Dan Rupple and Dave Toole
Sketches from the premier Christian comedy group

_____ **On the Edge #BK-B275** $15.95
by Steven James
A collection of 17 hard-hitting dramatic monologs

**These and other fine Meriwether Publishing books are available at
your local bookstore or direct from the publisher. Prices subject to
change without notice. Check our website or call for current prices.**

Name: _____ e-mail: _____

Organization name: _____

Address: _____

City: _____ State: _____

Zip: _____ Phone: _____

❑ **Check enclosed**

❑ **Visa / MasterCard / Discover #** _____

Signature: _____ Expiration date: _____
            (required for credit card orders)

Colorado residents: Please add 3% sales tax.
Shipping: Include $3.95 for the first book and 75¢ for each additional book ordered.

❑ *Please send me a copy of your complete catalog of books and plays.*

Order Form

Meriwether Publishing Ltd.
PO Box 7710
Colorado Springs CO 80933-7710
Phone: 800-937-5297 Fax: 719-594-9916
Website: www.meriwether.com

Please send me the following books:

_____ **Acts for God #BK-B274**   **$15.95**
by Howard Shirley
38 dramatic sketches for contemporary services

_____ **Worship Sketches 2 Perform #BK-B242**   **$15.95**
by Steven James
A collection of scripts for two actors

_____ **More Worship Sketches 2 Perform #BK-B258** **$14.95**
by Steven James
A collection of scripts for two actors

_____ **Service with a Smile #BK-B225**   **$14.95**
by Daniel Wray
52 humorous sketches for Sunday worship

_____ **More Service with a Smile #BK-B266**   **$15.95**
by Daniel Wray
Another helping of humorous sketches for Sunday worship

_____ **Isaac Air Freight: The Works #BK-B215**   **$16.95**
by Dan Rupple and Dave Toole
Sketches from the premier Christian comedy group

_____ **On the Edge #BK-B275**   **$15.95**
by Steven James
A collection of 17 hard-hitting dramatic monologs

These and other fine Meriwether Publishing books are available at your local bookstore or direct from the publisher. Prices subject to change without notice. Check our website or call for current prices.

Name: _____ e-mail: _____

Organization name: _____

Address: _____

City: _____ State: _____

Zip: _____ Phone: _____

❑ **Check enclosed**

❑ **Visa / MasterCard / Discover #** _____

Signature: _____   *Expiration date:* _____
(required for credit card orders)

Colorado residents: Please add 3% sales tax.
Shipping: Include $3.95 for the first book and 75¢ for each additional book ordered.

❑ *Please send me a copy of your complete catalog of books and plays.*

Order Form

Meriwether Publishing Ltd.
PO Box 7710
Colorado Springs CO 80933-7710
Phone: 800-937-5297 Fax: 719-594-9916
Website: www.meriwether.com

Please send me the following books:

_____ **Acts for God #BK-B274**   **$15.95**
by Howard Shirley
38 dramatic sketches for contemporary services

_____ **Worship Sketches 2 Perform #BK-B242**   **$15.95**
by Steven James
A collection of scripts for two actors

_____ **More Worship Sketches 2 Perform #BK-B258** **$14.95**
by Steven James
A collection of scripts for two actors

_____ **Service with a Smile #BK-B225**   **$14.95**
by Daniel Wray
52 humorous sketches for Sunday worship

_____ **More Service with a Smile #BK-B266**   **$15.95**
by Daniel Wray
Another helping of humorous sketches for Sunday worship

_____ **Isaac Air Freight: The Works #BK-B215**   **$16.95**
by Dan Rupple and Dave Toole
Sketches from the premier Christian comedy group

_____ **On the Edge #BK-B275**   **$15.95**
by Steven James
A collection of 17 hard-hitting dramatic monologs

These and other fine Meriwether Publishing books are available at
your local bookstore or direct from the publisher. Prices subject to
change without notice. Check our website or call for current prices.

Name: _____ e-mail: _____

Organization name: _____

Address: _____

City: _____ State: _____

Zip: _____ Phone: _____

❏ **Check enclosed**

❏ **Visa / MasterCard / Discover #** _____

Signature: _____   *Expiration*
                                                                  date: _____
(required for credit card orders)

Colorado residents: Please add 3% sales tax.
Shipping: Include $3.95 for the first book and 75¢ for each additional book ordered.

❏ *Please send me a copy of your complete catalog of books and plays.*